The
Starving
Artist's
Cookbook

The Starving Artist's Cookbook

Edgar Tharp
and
Robert E. Jaycoxe

Drawings by Barbara Carter

McGraw-Hill Book Company

New York • St. Louis • San Francisco • Auckland • Düsseldorf

Johannesburg • Kuala Lumpur • London • Mexico

Montreal • New Delhi • Panama • Paris • São Paulo

Singapore • Sydney • Tokyo • Toronto

123456789MUMU79876

Library of Congress Cataloging in Publication Data
Main entry under title:

The Starving artist's cookbook.

1. Cookery. I. Tharp, Edgar.
II. Jaycoxe, Robert E.
TX652.S67   641.5   75-33192
ISBN 0-07-063885-3

Contents

SOMETHING FROM THE BIRDS 49

FISH 54

MEATS 59

NOTE

Generally these recipes are for four persons, depending on appetite, age, voracity and current economic condition. With inflation, of course, that four will eventually grow to three.

PART ONE

An Artistic Approach to the Relief of Hunger and Other Things

The Need To Cook

. . . is mostly because you get hungry, and whether it's caused by falling off the booze or because you've lost the meal ticket that was the friend or chick who was letting you freeload, it's still a pretty painful process. The fat and overfed critics of art and literature allow as to how hunger historically is an incentive to creativity. Balls and thunderdash! There is hardly an artist or writer or sculptor who can lift his hand and make like a god without a full belly. So the need to cook exists to complement the need to create, particularly in a society where patrons of the arts are most conspicuous by their absence. Probably gone out to dinner at Antoine's. Of course, there's that other need that may be most pleasantly gratified by using cooking as a catalyst to pop a heretofore reluctant chick (or guy) into the sack.

But mainly it's because the artist, trying to exist and still create in the East or West Village in New York and similar places elsewhere, gets hungry. This is also true of the brethren and sisters from the provinces, who probably have a more difficult time of it surviving in the ghettos of San Francisco, Seattle, Chicago and Keokuk, Iowa. Their common denominator is an empty gut that needs filling on practically nothing. Thousands of cookbooks but not one to fit the starving artist's pocketbook or temperament. Well, in the immortal words of the poet Iver Lund,* "Here's how!"

This cookbook is aimed directly at Bohemia's "beat belly," with recipes designed to feed not one but four starving artists for two bucks a meal or less. The cost decreases as your ability to boost† becomes more skillful. All recipes are guaranteed and tested through years of trial by hunger in Greenwich Village and Soho. The prices are based on the lists of goodies provided by the A&P, Safeway and Pioneer (Where the Elite Buy Their Meat) supermarkets in New York City and should more or less average about the same around the country— well, who knows? Scrounging info comes first-hand from the Fulton Street fish markets and the wholesale produce markets on Manhattan's Lower East Side. The chapter on boosting is, of course, confidential, while that on booze-making comes from a long line of skeletons in the family closet dating back to the prohibition era.

Foreign cuisine comes, of course, from foreigners.

This ain't exactly cooking like Ma used to do, but then the old girl never did swing, now did she, man?

---

*Author of *The Mustard Plaster on the Old Man's Chest.*

†*Pilfer.*

Furnishing a Pad for Cooking

First things first. Pick up a mattress or a set of springs either from the street or from the Sally* Store. That basic need given a foundation, we can turn our attention to the belly.

Secondhand stores and the five and dime are the best bets for buying kitchenware and dishes for your pad. Pots and pans to begin with: at least two sauce-pans, one great big pot and a baking tin will do for openers. You'll need a frying pan, preferably a big (No. 8) black iron one, and some kind of a coffee pot, if you can't stand instant. Tools include a frenching knife, paring knife, spatula, a big wooden spoon and a can opener. Silver and some of the dishes you can boost from hamburger joints and restaurants. We'll take it for granted the landlord has provided a stove, sink and refrig.

Perhaps the most important item to start your kitchen with is a good collection of spices. They make the difference in cooking, so the expense is well justi-fied. Here's a basic list:

salt	garlic salt
black pepper	MSG

*Salvation Army.

oregano	paprika
basil	cinnamon
marjoram	crushed red pepper
chili powder	saffron
curry powder	nutmeg
dry mustard	bayleaf

Other basic seasonings and things include:

red-hot sauce	baking powder
soy sauce	baking soda
Worcestershire sauce	cornstarch
gravy coloring	dry yeast
vinegar	bread crumbs
olive oil	grated parmesan cheese

Staple items to keep in stock in the cupboard include coffee, sugar, flour, rice, potatoes, onions, cooking oil, spaghetti, noodles, some cans of tomato sauce or paste, canned or powdered milk, a gallon of red wine, candles and matches.

Straight* Shopping

This takes a lot of discipline because there are so many goodies displayed on the shelves that your rumbling gut is apt to make your eyes bigger than the two one-dollar bills in your hand. Of course, if your salivary glands become supersaturated and you just can't control yourself, you can always boost a jar of caviar or a filet mignon. But remember that this trip is primarily a buying trip, so try to stick to the items on your list.

Making a list and sticking to it is the secret of successful shopping. Thumb through the bible here and decide what you want to eat. Make a list of the necessary items for that meal, and then check the cupboard to see if any of them are in stock. If so, cross 'em off and apply the savings to a quart of beer or a jug of wine. Then head for the market with your list, taking the detour that avoids the bars. Buy exactly what it says on the list, then split the scene for the pad immediately before you blow the change.

The supermarket is the place to shop, despite the fact you may have a warm spot in your heart for the little independent corner deli or bodega. Canned stuff of all varieties is available in several sizes, and there's usually

*Legal.

something on sale. Buy the lesser-known or store brand of canned goods. They're cheaper and just as good. Vegetables can sometimes be had cheaper at the green–grocer next to the supermarket or from a street peddler, but as a rule the A&P–type places have the best buys. Likewise for meats, but the neighborhood fish market is the best place for finan haddie. It's always best to buy in quantities if the bread allows, particularly such staples as potatoes (10 pounds), onions (3), sugar (5), flour (5), and coffee (2 pounds or large instant). Spaghetti and noodles buy in the pound boxes and rice in a 2-pound box or 5-pound bag. Stay away from store-bought bread. If you don't make it yourself, buy it at an Italian or Polish bakery despite the fact that it will cost a few pennies more.

Outdoor Cooking

This is ridiculous. If you must, get a Boy Scout manual or hire a Girl Guide.

PART TWO

Hunger Relieved for Practically Nothing

Breakfasts

The first meal of the day is normally called breakfast, but that doesn't mean you have to get up before noon like straight people in order to partake. Breakfast is breakfast whether you have it at 2 P.M., the stroke of eight in the morning or at midnight, and many people prefer to indulge after the bars have closed. Breakfast may include anything from eggs and toast to caviar, black bread and sour cream washed down with iced vodka. But fish eggs are too far out of reach, and besides, they should be served in a satin-covered canopied bed by a scantily clad Greek Goddess (or God), so we'll come off that dream and stick to eggy type things. As Marcus Aurelius said, "Even in a Soho loft one can be happy."

Scrambled Eggs

2   *eggs per person*
dash of milk
dab of butter

This breakfast is so simple you can catch an extra few winks at the stove while doing it. Crack the eggs into a bowl, add a dash of milk and beat up. Heat the butter (oil may be used) in a skillet over a soft flame and then dump in the eggs and stir gently until done. Any eggy breakfast goes well with toast, home fries, bacon, ham, sausage or grits in any sort of combination.

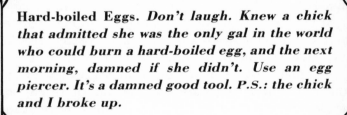

Hard-boiled Eggs. *Don't laugh. Knew a chick that admitted she was the only gal in the world who could burn a hard-boiled egg, and the next morning, damned if she didn't. Use an egg piercer. It's a damned good tool. P.S.: the chick and I broke up.*

Oatmeal

2   *cups oatmeal*
4   *cups water*
salt

This may bring back a childhood trauma or two but it will stick to your ribs. Besides, two bits worth of oats lasts a helluva long time. Dump the oats into the water. When it comes to a boil, let cook for a minute, stirring a bit. Turn off the gas, cover the pot and let it sit for about

five minutes. Oh yes, throw a pinch of salt in the water
before you boil it.

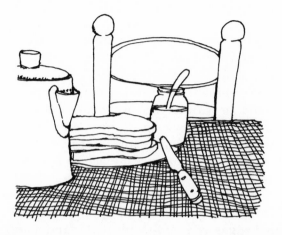

To Prevent Creaking of Bedsteads. *If your bedstead creaks at each movement of the sleeper,
remove the slats and wrap the ends of each in old
newspapers.*

Bedsteads That Still Creak. *If your bedstead still
creaks, let it.*

French Toast

    6   *slices stale bread*
  4-6   *eggs*
    1   *cup milk or light cream*
        pinch of salt
    1   *cup shortening*
        butter

powdered sugar
maple or simple syrup*

A good cheap breakfast. Mostly stuff you'll have around the house anyway. Use bread two days old. Trim the crust and combine all ingredients except sugar and syrup and whip well. Put bread in shallow dish and pour mixture over bread. Turn if necessary. Be sure to use a spatula and be careful not to break. Let soak for ten minutes. Hell, just soak up all the mixture and fry over a moderate heat slowly till a golden brown on both sides. (Knew a chick like that once.) Place on a paper towel for a second to absorb grease. Trick here is to put all the toast on a serving platter and place in preheated oven (350°) until toast begins to puff up. Sprinkle lightly with powdered sugar and serve with butter and maple syrup.

For Fancy-Pants Guests: Cut bread in a circle when wet. (An old coffee can is great for this.) Cook as above and add a touch of cinnamon on top of the powdered sugar. Crazy.

Is it one of those real lazy Sunday mornings? Add juice, country sausages and coffee and serve it to her in bed. A liberated breakfast.

Pancakes

1   *cup all-purpose flour*
1   *egg, beaten*
1   *cup milk*
1½ *tsp baking powder*
2   *tsp sugar*
½   *tsp salt*
1   *TB melted butter, oil or shortening*

*Simple syrup: sugar melted in hot water to taste.

Sometimes called hotcakes, griddle cakes or flap–jacks, they taste just as good no matter what the name. If you like, you can make the batter the night before and store in the refrigerator to save time in the morning. To make, sift all the dry ingredients together. Add the milk and then the egg and melted butter and mix well, but leave it a little lumpy. Drop batter on hot greased griddle or fry pan. When cakes have risen, are full of bubbles and cooked around the edges, flip them over. Serve immediately with butter and syrup, sugar, jam or jelly.

To Destroy Cockroaches. *Sprinkle hellebore on the floor at night. They eat it and are poisoned.*

It is certain that a good constitution must necessarily be the foundation of a long life.

Vegetables

TABLE FOR BOILING VEGETABLES

Vegetables	Boiling Time (Min)	Vegetables	Boiling Time (Min)
asparagus tips	5 to 15	beans, lima, navy,	
asparagus butts	10 to 20	kidney	20 to 25
beans, green	15 to 25	beet greens	5 to 15

Vegetables	Boiling Time (Min)	Vegetables	Boiling Time (Min)
beets, whole	30 to 45	parsnips, cut up	10 to 15
broccoli	8 to 15	peas	10 to 20
brussels sprouts	6 to 15	potatoes, white	25 to 40
cabbage	3 to 8	potatoes, sweet	25 to 35
carrots	15 to 25	pumpkin, cut up	20 to 30
cauliflower flowers	8 to 10	rutabaga, cut up	20 to 30
cauliflower, whole	15 to 20	spinach	3 to 10
celery, cut up	15 to 20	squash, cut up	5 to 15
corn on the cob	10 to 20	tomatoes, whole	5 to 15
cucumbers	5 to 10	turnips, cut up	10 to 20
eggplant, cut up	8 to 12	zucchini, cut up	5 to 10
onions, whole	20 to 30		

Milkweed Shoots

½-1   *lb milkweed shoots*
butter
salt and pepper

The common milkweed (*Asclepias syriaca*) is another wild plant that nature nuts have been eating for years. You can't buy them in the market, so take a weekend hike in the country in the spring or visit Grandma's farm. Best time is late spring: that's when the first shoots begin to appear. Cut those that are 6 to 8 inches long and still young enough to snap when bent. Wash well and cook, covered, in a little salted water for 10 minutes. Drain and add butter and salt and pepper. Milkweed may also be served like asparagus, with mayonnaise or on toast covered with hollandaise sauce.

Dandelion Greens

large bunch of greens
small piece salt pork cut in 1" squares

4 *potatoes, peeled and quartered*
salt to taste

Even Euell Gibbons would approve of this tasty, economical and nutritious wild plant food. Go out in the front yard or wherever and pick yourself a big bunch of dandelion greens. Try to get the ones the dog missed. If possible, pick the youngest and most tender plants, and then wash the leaves thoroughly. To cook, bring 1½ quarts of water to a rolling boil and drop in the greens and salt pork. Turn down the heat and simmer for an hour. During the last half–hour add the spuds and salt to taste. If you like, add a little vinegar for extra flavor when serving. Even the juice that the leaves of the *Taraxacum officinale* are cooked in is tasty and nutritious.

Pennsylvania Dutch Red Cabbage

1   *TB cooking oil*
2   *cups shredded red cabbage*
1   *apple (not peeled), cubed*
2   *TB vinegar*
2   *TB water*
½   *tsp salt*
¼   *tsp caraway seed (optional)*

This is a real Dutch treat, and if you like, you can substitute regular green cabbage, but it won't be quite as Dutchy. Heat the oil in a saucepan. Add the rest of the stuff and cover tightly. Cook 10 to 15 minutes over low heat, stirring now and then. Eat.

Green Beans Greenwich Village

1   *lb green beans*
2   *qt water*
    dash of salt

This, next to spuds, is *the* basic vegetable except for old onion. Cut off the ends of the beans, wash, then cut in two. Put in a pot of water, throw in a dash of salt and cook for about 15 to 25 minutes. Don't overcook. Green beans go great with any meal. Also you can eat them cold or make a salad of them. If you can't get fresh green beans, or are in a hurry, buy a large can and heat them up gently for about 5 minutes.

Sweet and Sour Green Beans

1   *can green beans*
2   *slices bacon, diced*

1   *small onion, finely chopped*
1   *TB flour*
¼   *cup vinegar*
2   *TB sugar*
    salt and pepper (½ tsp each)

This really perks up the old green bean, sort of giving it a Chinese flavor. Fry the bacon until crisp in a fry pan. Remove bacon and throw in the onion and cook until golden. Stir in flour. Add the bean juice and all other ingredients except the beans and quickly bring to a boil. Reduce heat and add green beans. Let beans cook until thoroughly heated (3 to 5 minutes), stirring all the while. Serve with the bits of bacon sprinkled over the top.

Free-form Tomatoes and Okra

1   *lb okra*   *salt and pepper*
1   *large can tomatoes*   ¼   *tsp basil*
1   *onion, chopped*

If you're a Damn Yankee, you may have to learn to like this, for it's purely a Southern dish. Sauté the onion in the fry pan for 5 minutes, then add the okra and sauté for 5 more minutes. Then stir in the tomatoes, basil and salt and pepper. Cook over low heat for 15 minutes.

If fresh okra is not available, use canned, but add it and the rest of the stuff after the onion has been sautéed.

Beets and Beet Greens

1   *bunch beets with tops*
1   *TB vinegar*

This is a two-in-one vegetable. If you don't want beets and greens at the same time, save one or the other and cook another day. Cut the tops from the beets and save. Wash the beets and cook in a large pot of water 30 to 45 minutes. Drain, remove the skins and then either slice or dice or eat them whole. The vinegar is to put in the water while boiling to keep the good red color.

For the greens, wash and discard the tough stems and leaves and cook in a small amount of water for 5 to 15 minutes. Serve with vinegar.

Name This One

potatoes	*butter*
carrots	*parsley*

Next time you're making potatoes and carrots as vegetables for your dinner, try this. After boiling them, mix them together in a warm bowl and add water (not milk) and lots of butter. Mash—or mix with an electric blender, if you're lucky enough to have one. Top with a bit of butter and freshly chopped parsley, and serve in a warmed covered bowl. Let 'em guess. Carrots add color, and parsley makes grand contrast.

NOTE: Make a large pattie with any leftover, brown in fry pan and serve with a soft fried egg on top. A great breakfast dish as well.

Red Radishes

1	*bunch radish*	*butter*
	ice	*salt*

Always been crazy about radishes. However, the

feeling was never mutual till we started eating them this way. Take a bunch of radish, clean well and cut leaves off, leaving a little stem to pick them up with. Put in a bowl of cold water, pack with ice and chill in fridge. Serve in small individual bowls (in the cold water). Pick up a radish by its stem, cut it in half, add a bit of butter to each half with a dash of salt. Presto—*no burp*! Don't know why it works but it does.

White Radishes

1   *bunch white radish*   *olive oil*
    salt   *wine vinegar or white*

Slice radish in thin slices. Place on platter and separate in individual pieces. Sprinkle lightly with salt and chill in fridge. Place slices on small individual plate and add olive oil and a touch of vinegar before serving. Makes a great little dish of something extra. Salt sweats it out.

Cauliflower

1   *head cauliflower*   *salt*

Remove the leaves and wash carefully. Break into fleurettes and cook in salted water for 8 to 10 minutes. If you leave it whole, cook from 15 to 20 minutes. Serve buttered or with a sauce.

Mashed Potatoes

4   *medium potatoes,*   *milk*
     peeled and quartered   *salt and pepper*
3   *TB butter or marge*

This is an all-time favorite for just about everybody. Boil the potatoes and drain. Add butter, salt and pepper and start mashing with a masher, or you can use a fork. Add milk gradually until the spuds have the texture you desire. Use a fork at the very last and whip energetically until all the lumps are gone.

For leftover mashed potatoes, add a dash of black pepper, a small amount of chopped onion (depending on how much mashed potatoes you have), a splash of water and a shot of flour to make a large pattie. Brown in a fry pan with a little oil. Makes a great breakfast or lunch dish.

Potato Pancakes. *Make these the way you usually do, but do not grate,* shred fine. *Made this way they will taste better, feel crisper and have maximum flavor. Otherwise stick to Mom's old recipe.* Makes some difference—*but don't tell her.*

Wild or Brown Rice

1   *cup wild or brown rice*
2   *cups water*
1   *tsp salt*
     dab of butter or marge

This is the good rice with a lot of nutritional value. In a saucepan, bring the water to the boil and add rice slowly. Reduce heat, add salt and butter. Cover and simmer for about an hour or until all the water has been absorbed.

Glazed Carrots

6-8   *small carrots, slightly undercooked*
  3   *TB oil*
  5   *TB brown or white sugar*

This type of carrot goes particularly well with birds—or if you have a sweet tooth. Heat the oil in a fry pan over low heat. Add carrots, sprinkle with sugar and cook until they are brown. Then add a small amount of water and cook until well glazed, turning as necessary.

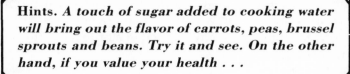

Hints. *A touch of sugar added to cooking water will bring out the flavor of carrots, peas, brussel sprouts and beans. Try it and see. On the other hand, if you value your health . . .*

Zesty Carrots

4	*large carrots, scraped and washed*
2	*TB grated onion*
2	*TB horseradish*
½	*cup mayonnaise*
	dash of pepper and salt
2	*TB melted butter or marge*
¼	*cup dry bread crumbs*

This is an old Shaker recipe and makes a fine side dish for almost any meat, fish or fowl. Cut the carrots in half and then into thin strips, julienne style. In a sauce–pan, add enough water to just cover the carrots, then cook, covered, for 6 or 8 minutes. In a bowl, combine the onion, horseradish, mayonnaise, salt and pepper, and ¼ cup of the water you cooked the carrots in. Place the carrots in a small baking dish and pour the other ingredients over the carrots, spreading about evenly. Sprinkle bread crumbs over the top and bake for 15 minutes in a 375° oven.

Cabbage

Gets down to 15¢ a pound sometimes and as such is a real basic item in anyone's Class C diet. Boil it, man, for the easiest and best results. Cut the head in quarters and boil in a big pot of salted water for about 30 minutes. Comes in a lovely pastel green or red and is not only decorative but delicious with salt and pepper and butter or vinegar. Leftovers may be fried in a little oil or thrown into a soup.

Other uses:

Cole slaw (see Salads).

Stuffed cabbage.

Cabbage soup (obvious).

Scalloped Potatoes

8	*potatoes*	*some flour*
1	*onion*	*dab of margarine*
	milk	

This is a real change of pace if you're on a potato diet. Costs from 15 to 20 cents. Peel and slice the spuds thin (use a vegetable slicer-grater if you have one). In a greased casserole place a layer of potatoes and a few slices of onion. Salt and pepper them and add a little garlic powder, then sprinkle with flour and put a dab of marge on top. A little grated cheese added to each layer and the top, plus a little shot of paprika on the top, give

Leftover Vegetables. *Don't ever throw these away. Great for stuffing meat loafs and omelets.*

it added zing. Build up as many layers as you have potatoes and then fill with milk to the top of the last layer. Bake in a medium oven (375°) for about two hours.

Basic Dried Bean Recipe

(*for*: Navy, Lima, Kidney, or Pinto Beans)

1	*cup beans*		or
1	*qt water*	4	*slices bacon, cut up*
2	*small onions, chopped*		*salt and pepper*
⅛	*lb salt pork, cut up*		

Dried beans, or "poop seed," as they are sometimes called by the less sensitive among us, will fill you full of protein as well as a bit of sulphur dioxide (known as taking the good with the bad), but the latter inconvenience is just another one of those ill winds that eventually subside. So do those around you.

Boil the salt pork about 10 minutes. Pick and wash the beans well. Then dump everything into the pot, bring to a boil, lower the heat and simmer about one hour or until beans are tender. (If you soak the beans overnight they will not need to cook so long.)

White Beans à la Française

2	*TB olive oil*
½	*tsp oregano*
1	*fresh tomato, diced*
1	*16-oz can white beans, drained*
	salt and pepper to taste

1 *TB chopped parsley*
1 *clove of garlic, crushed*

Lightly sauté garlic in oil. Add oregano, tomato and a little of the bean liquid. Drain off rest of bean liquid. Simmer covered 5 minutes. Add beans and parsley and salt and pepper to taste. Cook till beans are hot. A dish that's ready in no time and rich in vitamins, minerals and body-building proteins. A 16-oz can of beans costs 35 cents. What more can you ask? The small perto beans are great for this and a spot of tabasco gives it a nice lift.

Xmas Decor. *Dip pieces of yarn in a flour-and-water paste, then crisscross over inflated balloons of different sizes and shapes. Let dry, deflate balloons and clean. Attach wire, hang them somewhere and spray them with different colors—silver, gold, etc. They make unusual xmas decorations. Pretty cheap and you damned sure can't buy these anywhere.*

Hamburger

Hamburger à la Guido

1   *lb hamburger*   *oregano*
    salt   *romano cheese*
    pepper

Guido Giampieri is famous not only for the booze he serves at the Kettle of Fish on McDougal Street in

Greenwich Village but also for his fine Italian cuisine.
Make 8 thin patties from the hamburger, salt and pepper
them and add a dash of oregano on each patty. Then put
a slice of romano between two patties, sandwich style,
so you have four all together. Heat up the oven and broil
to your taste. This goes well with a simple spaghetti, and
if you're loaded (with money, that is), have a salad and
some *vino* on the side. If you're loaded in the other
sense, better eat some hamburgers.

Hamburger Creole

1	*lb hamburger*	1	*green pepper*
1	*small can cut okra*	1	*onion*
	tomato paste		

Hungry Cajuns in the audience will appreciate this
old New Orleans dish. Economywise it costs about 80
cents (keeping in mind, of course, what may be left in
the cupboard before you shop or what is boostable).
Chop up the onion and pepper and sauté in a dab of olive

Hamburger Press. *A must tool in my house.
Make one out of old coffee can open on both
ends. Cut some plastic inserts, a little smaller
than can opening. Put foil on bottom, put in
insert, hamburger and another insert on top.
Press down till tight. Repeat. Freeze with inserts. To use, place a knife between hamburgers
and give a slight twist, and they pop out uniform
and nicely shaped.*

oil. Crumple up the hamburg and brown in the same fry pan, then dump in the okra and tomato paste and about three tomato paste cans full of water. Sort of stir it around and then let simmer from 15 to 20 minutes. Seasoning should include salt and pepper, garlic salt, marjoram, a dash of Worcestershire and a couple of shots of Louisiana "red devil" to hotten it up. Goes well with a side dish of rice, hot biscuits and a green salad.

Paul's Cannibalburgers

1½   *lb hamburger*   *loaf of rye*

If you haven't eaten for several days and suddenly raise an ace and can't wait to get back to the pad to cook, this is a great way to placate the gut with a shot of raw protein. Get the stuff at the supermarket and duck into the nearest bar or find the closest park bench. Mold the meat into four patties, borrow salt and pepper and hot sauce from the barkeep, and build sandwiches. In the park you'll have to forgo the seasoning. Throw the extra rye to the pigeons in the park, or if you're in the bar, drink it up!

Cloths for Dusting. *Saturate dust cloths (cotton flannel is good) with kerosene and ½ teaspoon lemon oil for cleaning odor. Let soak overnight in a covered jar. Wring out and dry, then use. Clean and wash when dirty. Repeat procedure. What do you think the commercial guys use? Regular cloths?*

Hamburger Steak

1   *lb hamburger*   4   *toothpicks*
4   *slices bacon*

This is another "fast feast" unless you're a baked potato nut. Cut the hamburger in half and form into 1"-thick round steaks which are flat top and bottom. With toothpicks secure the bacon slices (2 to a steak) on the sides of the burger so they completely encircle the steak. Stick under the broiler for 5 minutes for each side. If you want a fast meal, open a can of vegetables (green beans, corn, etc.) and a box of frozen french fries and start cooking on top of the stove the same time you begin to broil the steaks. It'll all be done at the same time.

Hamburger, Potato, Celery and Onion Dinner

1   *lb hamburger*
2   *small onions, sliced*
4   *potatoes, peeled and quartered*
1½   *cups beef bouillon*
4   *stalks celery, cut in 1-inch pieces*

Hamburgers. *Can be made uniform in size with an old coffee can. Just use open end to cut and closed end to flatten. It cuts down on arguments with the kids.*

½   tsp oregano
    salt and pepper

You could call this hamburger stew, but somehow
that name just doesn't seem to fit. Anyway, in the big
skillet or fry pan, sauté the onions and push to one side.
Then brown the meat. Throw in the bouillon, bring to a
boil and turn heat to low. Add the rest of the stuff, cover
and simmer for 20 minutes, or until spuds are done.

Hamburger Gravy

1	lb hamburger	2	TB cornstarch or flour
4-8	potatoes	2	TB gravy coloring
1	onion		

With hamburger at about half a buck a throw and
the spuds going for about a dime, you can afford another
vegetable and a salad and maybe even a bowl of
J*E*L*L*O. Over a low flame, crumple up the hamburger in the skillet. Chop up the onion and throw it in, and
stir everything about until the meat is browned. Salt and
pepper, and then add two cups of water and stir until it
boils. Stir in about two tablespoons of cornstarch or
flour to thicken and add two tablespoons of gravy
coloring. A dash of Worcestershire and a taste of garlic
salt help the flavor. Let it simmer a bit, then serve over
either boiled or mashed potatoes.

Stuffed Green Peppers

4	green peppers	½	cup rice
½	lb hamburger	1	egg, beaten
1	onion, chopped	⅓	cup milk

½   tsp salt   ½   cup bread crumbs
1   cup hot water

If you want to "hot" this up a bit you'll have to add some unstuffed pepper—black, red or cayenne. Brown the hamburger. Cut cap from stern end of each pepper, remove seeds and parboil the peppers for 10 minutes. Chop up the caps of the peppers and sauté gently with the rice and onion. Add all the other stuff, except the water, and mix well and then shove it all into the peppers. Put the peppers in a baking dish and pour 1 inch of hot water around them. Bake at 375° for about ¾ hour, basting frequently. Not too bad once you get used to it.

Daisy's Meat Loaf

1   lb hamburger
1   egg
1   large onion, finely chopped
4   slices of bread, decrusted
1   cup milk
1   small can tomato sauce

Cleaning Aluminum Pots. *Just stew some tomatoes or make a good tomato sauce in the pot and watch the difference. Cleans aluminum like new. Rhubarb, tart apples, sour milk, cream of tartar, tomato juice or buttermilk will do the same thing. Leaving food in aluminum pots causes the metal to become pitted or dark.*

Even with inflation this will cost well under two bucks, and it makes enough so you can either invite a hungry friend or make sandwiches the next day for lunch. With your hands, mix all the ingredients together, except the tomato sauce, plus a little salt and pepper. If the mixture is a little too stiff, add another dab of milk. Mold into a loaf and place in a baking tin. Pour the tomato sauce over the top, and carefully add a tomato sauce can of water, making sure you don't wash the tomato sauce off the top of the loaf. Bake in a 300° oven for about an hour and a half. This makes its own gravy, and seeing as how you have the oven going anyway, bake a couple of potatoes to go along with it.

Sandy's Chili

1	*lb hamburger*	3	*onions, chopped*
2	*cans red kidney beans*	3	*TB chili powder*
1	*large can tomatoes*	1	*bay leaf*
1	*small can tomato paste*		

Brown hamburger in a large pot. Throw in all the rest of the stuff and stir it up good. Let it simmer for about an hour. This goes great with corn bread and salad. If you want the chili hotter, dose it up with some Louisiana red pepper sauce.

Macaroni Supreme

½ lb hamburger
1 cup macaroni
1 small onion, sliced
1 small can tomatoes
1 small can mushroom bits

½ cup grated "rat"
   cheese
   salt and pepper
½ tsp oregano

No starving Italian artist ever had a dish like this, only you lucky, starving American artists! Cook the macaroni first. Brown hamburger, and add the tomatoes, onion, macaroni and season. Stir and cook for about five minutes (low heat) until it's all well blended. Add cheese and mushrooms and continue cooking and stirring until the cheese is melted. A snap.

Macaroni Italiano

½ cup macaroni
½ lb hamburger
1 small green pepper, chopped
1 small onion, chopped
2 small cans tomato sauce
½ cup grated parmesan cheese

Stained Silver. *Salt will remove the stain from silver caused by eggs, when applied with a soft cloth.*

> salt and pepper
½   tsp oregano

They call this something else in Italian, but it tastes just as good over here, particularly served with salad with Italian dressing, bread and *vino*. Cook the macaroni first. Brown the hamburger, and then combine all the rest of the ingredients. Stick it in a greased casserole dish and bake at 325° for one hour.

Spaghetti Meat Sauce

½	lb hamburger		olive oil
1	large can tomatoes	½	tsp oregano
1	small can tomato paste	¼	tsp garlic salt
1	onion, chopped	¼	tsp salt
1	green pepper, chopped	¼	tsp black pepper

If you cook the spaghetti at the same time you make the sauce, you can have a complete meal (including a salad, garlic bread and *vino*) in about 20 minutes. However, the sauce is a lot tastier if you let her cook for at least an hour. To make, brown the hamburger in a fry pan and at the same time sauté the onion and green pepper separately in the olive oil. When the hamburger

---

Squeaking Doors. *Oil the hinges with a drop or two from the sewing machine oil can.*

is brown and the pepper and onion done, about 5 minutes, add the peppers and onion to the hamburger along with the rest of the stuff except the tomato paste. Cook over a low heat for 5 minutes more, stirring all the while, and then stir in the tomato paste. Let it simmer, stirring every 10 minutes or so, for at least an hour longer. If possible, age the sauce a day or so (covered) in the refrigerator before using.

Stews

Lamb Stew

2 *lb breast of lamb*
1 *lb carrots*
8 *potatoes (at least)*
1 *onion or so*
1 *can sweet peas*
1 *can tomato sauce*

This will really stick to your ribs, particularly in the winter, and you can build on it* and, like, make it last forever. Bless the Lamb Growers Association for pushing their stuff, for this cut costs from 13 to 19 cents a pound. Total cost should run around six bits.

Slice the breast off two ribs thick and throw in the big pot. Add the vegetables whole or cut into large pieces, cover with salted water and boil softly until the vegetables are done. Scoop off the excess lamb fat, add the peas and tomato sauce and simmer for another hour. Seasoning should include salt and pepper, garlic powder, a dash of hot sauce, a bay leaf and anything else your imagination comes up with. Thicken with corn—starch or flour after about a half an hour of simmering. Hot biscuits with this are a boon to gravy soppers. To

*Add to it.

build on a lamb stew when it's nearly depleted, boil additional vegetables separately, add to the pot with some of the vegetable water, season again, thicken and simmer. This may be repeated any number of times, but after a while you'll get pretty damn sick of lamb stew.

Black Bean Glop

1	*lb black beans*	1	*large onion, cut up*
1	*lb stewing beef*	3	*cloves garlic, diced*
¼	*lb salt pork*		*salt and pepper*

This is an old Missouri recipe and everybody just

To Soften Putty. *A red-hot iron will soften old putty so that it can be easily removed.*

calls it Black Bean Glop. Not knowing exactly where to put it in the book and seeing as how we have no section for "Glop," we arbitrarily stuck it under "Stew." It's damn good, nutritious and cheap.

Cut the beef into bite-size pieces and the salt pork into three or four pieces. Combine all the ingredients in a large pot and cover with water. Cook for ½ hour at high heat and then simmer covered for about three hours. Check it once in a while and add a little boiling water to the pot if needed. The beans are done if when you blow on them the skin splits. The meat will be done at the same time. Serve over rice, with either corn bread or hot biscuits on the side.

Irish Seven-Course Dinner. *A six-pack of beer and one boiled potato seasoned to taste.*

Casseroles

Tuna Fish

1	*can tuna*	1	*can peas*
1	*can mushroom soup*	¼	*lb noodles*

This is a quickie that will really satisfy your primary appetite. A small can of tuna runs from 24 cents to about 40, with the lesser known brands the best bargains. Peas go for about two bits, soup 20¢ and noodles about 20¢. Boil the noodles in salted water for 10 minutes. Drain and mix in the other things, and season with salt, pepper and garlic powder. Be sure to add the pea juice so the mixture will be moist enough. Dump the whole mess into a buttered casserole dish, sprinkle the top with paprika and bake in a hot oven for 15 or 20 minutes. If there's a chick about, hot biscuits, salad and a taste of wine should entice her to provide the dessert.

Filet of Sole Casserole

1   *lb filet of sole (about 4 slices)*
1   *can peas*
1   *can stewed tomatoes*
1   *onion*

A fifth of chablis makes this meal complete. The price of a sole fluctuates, but in this case it generally runs well under a piece of silver. Roll up each slice of sole, place in a casserole dish with a dab of butter on top of each roll, salt and pepper, sprinkle on some paprika and bake in a hot oven (400°) for 15 minutes. Chop up the onion and sauté in butter or oil. Thicken the pea juice with a couple of tablespoons of cornstarch or flour, and add to the onions along with the peas and tomatoes. Simmer about 5 minutes, then dump the whole works over the fish and pop the casserole back into the oven for another 5 minutes. You should really make a fishy night of it by buying the chablis by the gallon, if you've got the bread.

Chicken Tettrazini

4	*cups cooked chicken, diced*	3	*scallions, chopped*
¼	*lb mushrooms, sliced*	½	*lb cooked spaghetti*
1	*small onion, chopped*	1	*cup cream*
		2	*TB cooking wine*

This really ought to go under the heading of Italian food, but the editor figured we already had enough of that sort of stuff, and he has a mean look. Anyway, sauté the mushrooms and onions in butter or a little oil. In a separate pan, simmer the cream and wine for about 3 minutes, then add the chicken, scallions, onions and mushrooms. Simmer the whole mess for another 5 minutes. Put the spaghetti in a buttered casserole dish, pour the rest of the mixed ingredients over it and heat in a 350° oven until bubbling (about 20 minutes). Like most casseroles, this is a one-dish meal. Maybe a salad, some bread and a little *vino*.

Upside-down Chili Pie

Sandy's Chili	1 *small can cream-*
(see "Hamburger")	*style corn*
1 *12-oz pkg corn*	1 *egg*
muffin mix	¼ *cup milk*

Make the chili as prescribed. In a bowl, combine all the other ingredients for a regular muffin mix. Place chili in a casserole and pour muffin mix evenly over it. Bake in a medium oven (325°) for about 25 minutes, or until top is golden brown. Let stand in casserole for a few minutes, then invert onto a serving platter.

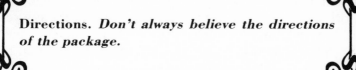

Directions. *Don't always believe the directions of the package.*

Boston Baked Beans

2	cups navy beans	1	tsp prepared mustard
¼	to ½ lb salt pork	1	TB molasses
1	tsp salt	1	TB sugar

This recipe is as old as Boston itself and is one of the reasons they used to refer to Bostonians as "The Windy Folk." Wash the beans, cover with water and boil for 2 minutes. Remove from heat and let stand 1 hour. Cover and cook slowly until tender. Drain and save bean water. Put half the beans in a bean pot, add the salt pork, then the rest of the beans. Dissolve the mustard, salt, sugar and molasses in a little hot water and pour over beans. Add enough of the bean water to completely cover the windberries. Cover and bake for about 8 hours in a 275° oven. Add water occasionally as needed, preferably hot water.

Pork Chops

4	chops		milk
8	potatoes	1	onion

This is merely scalloped potatoes* with a pork chop

*See "Vegetables."

or two stuck between the various layers of spuds. Bake about two hours in a medium-high oven (400°). The pork flavor permeating the potatoes makes them a real taste treat. Shoulder pork chops are the cheapest buy. You should be able to get at least six plus the potatoes for less than two dollars and maybe even squeeze in a green salad or a tomato to slice.

When gnats collect themselves before the setting of the sun and form a vortex in the shape of a column, it announces fine weather.

Something from the Birds

Fried Chicken

1   *2-lb frying chicken, cut up*   1   *cup oil*

This bird is about the cheapest buy on the market, from 25 cents a pound and up. Heat the oil (preferably olive) over a gentle flame, and then throw in the chicken parts after they have been subjected to a salt and pepper treatment. Cook slowly, turning often, until golden brown. Side dishes should include either french fries or rice, a green vegetable and salad.

Roast Chicken

1   *2½- to 4-lb roasting chicken*
     stuffing (see p. 53)

You may not have a car in your garage, but you can damn well afford to park this bird in your oven. Preheat the oven to 325°, stuff the bird and roast for from 2 to 3 hours, basting every 20 or 30 minutes. If you want gravy, put the pan the bird was cooked in on top of a burner on the stove over low heat. Stir in a cup of boiling water. Add a little salt and pepper and thicken with cornstarch or flour, stirring in a tablespoon of Kitchen Bouquet at the very last.

Broiled Chicken

1   *1½- to 2-lb broiler*
1   *stick margarine or butter, melted*
    salt and pepper

Next to frying, this is just about the simplest way there is to prepare chicken. Split the bird in half lengthwise, brush the halves with the melted margarine or butter and season with salt and pepper. Place the chicken skin side down in a shallow pan and about six inches below the heat of the broiler. Broil slowly for 20 minutes, brushing with melted butter as needed. Turn over and broil the skin side for another 10 to 15 minutes—longer if you like it crispy brown.

Aluminum Foil. *Put aluminum foil on shelves inside kitchen cabinets. Reflects light and is easy to clean: just wipe with a damp cloth. (First line wooden shelves with paper to keep foil from sticking.)*

Chicken à la King

1 *cup cooked chicken, diced*   *salt and pepper*
1 *can mushroom soup*   *buttered toast*

This is great for a quick lunch, plus it gives you a way to use up your leftover chicken. Throw everything except the toast into a saucepan and cook over a low heat from 5 to 10 minutes, stirring frequently. Pour it over the toast and you're in business.

Chicken and Dumplings

1 *1½- to 2-lb chicken, cut up*
   simple dumplings (see p. 65)
   salt and pepper

This old Depression standby still serves its function in what is now *called* a Recession. (I mean, who's kidding who, right?) It's cheap, filling, and nothing is wasted, because you save the stock to make soup with.

Put the chicken in a large pot filled with at least 2 quarts of water, add a dash of salt and pepper and bring to a boil. Turn the heat to low, and cook 30 to 40 minutes, or until tender. Drop the dumplings into the pot for the last 15 minutes.

Chicken Fricassee

1	*2- to 3-lb chicken*	*flour*
1	*cup cream or milk*	*salt and pepper*

This chicken comes out so tender the meat practically falls off the bone. Cut the bird up and roll the parts in the flour seasoned with the salt and pepper. In a large skillet, brown well on all sides. Pour in the cream or milk, and cook, covered, until tender. Make a gravy with the leftover milk sauce by thickening with a little flour or cornstarch and adding a tablespoon of Kitchen Bouquet for coloring and extra seasoning. Serve with mashed potatoes and a green vegetable.

Roast Turkey

You can't afford this, so make up with your parents or inlaws (temporarily) and go home for Thanksgiving.

Live chastely if you wish to live long. On the other hand, if you wish to really live . . .

Roast Goose

See "Roast Turkey."

Broiled Squab

First you go to the park and nab a pigeon. . . .

Stuffing

4   cups ½-inch-cubed dry bread
¼   cup celery, chopped
1   small onion, chopped
1   egg, slightly beaten
½   stick margarine or butter
1   tsp salt
¼   tsp pepper
½   tsp sage
1   to 1½ cups boiling water

This is what makes the bird. There are many variations, but this is the basic stuffing and you can't go wrong. Add the seasonings, celery and onion to the bread and mix. Melt the margarine or butter in the boiling water and gently mix in the bread, then mix in the egg. This is enough to stuff a 3½- to 4-pound bird.

> *When it rains plentifully in May, it generally rains but little in September. And the contrary.*

Fish

Arturo's Fish Cakes

¼	lb flaked bacalao (fresh dry cod)	1	rib celery
¾	lb potatoes (2 or 3)	3	TB corn oil
½	parsnip, fresh	1	TB dry mustard
1	medium onion		white pepper (ground)
1	small turnip	3	eggs, raw

Bring pot of water to a boil and turn down. Put flaked fish in a strainer and poach in pot for 5 minutes. Remove and drain, set aside. Cut all vegetables fine and boil. Drain and mash fine in large bowl with 3 tablespoons of oil. Mix and mash with three raw eggs and the fish, and add seasoning. Make into small balls. Put in a heavily flowered flat cookie pan and refrigerate overnight. Before cooking, reflour and reshape fish balls. Fry in pan in 1 inch of fairly hot oil. Balls will rise. When brown, remove and drain. About 3 minutes. Add this to a simple pasta dish and you're home free. A real good, inexpensive meal. Even better served as an hors d'oeuvre, or separate dish. No salt! And do this recipe step by step.

Shrimp Creole

1   *lb raw, shelled shrimp*
1   *onion, chopped*
1   *green pepper, chopped*
2   *stalks (not bunches) celery, chopped*
2   *large tomatoes, chopped*
1   *cup chicken broth (chicken bouillon cube will do)*
2   *oz cooking wine*
    salt
    tabasco
    bay leaf

Fish and Chips. Watch this one in places you're not too sure of. You'll be surprised at how many times you're eating shark meat or skate. Not too bad either.

This may stretch the two-dollar budget, but it's just as good if not better than anything that ever came out of New Orleans. So splurge. Sauté onions, green pepper and celery, preferably in bacon fat, if you have it. Add tomatoes, the cup of broth, wine, a pinch of salt, dash of tabasco and the bay leaf, and simmer 45 minutes, stirring occasionally. Add the shrimp and simmer another 6 or 7 minutes. Serve with rice, and drink up the rest of the cooking wine.

Baked Shark Steaks

2	lb shark meat	½	cup bread crumbs
½	cup flour	½	cup dry white
	olive or cooking oil		vermouth
¼	cup chopped shallots		salt
	or scallions		pepper
½	tsp oregano		sprig parsley

Cut fish into 1½-inch steaks, remove any skin and wash in cold water. Dry well, salt and pepper it and lightly flour both sides. In hot oil, brown fish lightly on both sides and transfer to a baking dish. Save frying oil for basting. Sprinkle herbs and scallions (we prefer shallots) over fish. Add a layer of bread crumbs and a dot of butter on each steak. Pour in vermouth and bake in an oven 350° (preheated) until fork pierces easily.

About 25 minutes. Do not overcook. While cooking, baste with a little frying oil. Sprinkle with parsley and serve with rice, green beans and sliced lemon. Guests bring the white wine, of course. Only fair.

All young sharks are good to eat: fillet, or cut into steaks, and boiled, broiled or baked. Use white meat only. Best types are mako, sandbar, soupfin. Leave the old one alone. We like it but don't know how they make that soupfin soup. Wow.

Clam Fritters

1	can minced clams (save liquid)	1	egg
¾	cup milk	1	TB oil
1	cup flour	1	tsp baking powder

Add clam liquid to milk: makes about 1 cup. Whip all together and chill for ½ hour (improves taste). Drip off spoon into hot oil and serve with tomato ketchup in a center bowl. Big question asked here is: How do you make the sauce? Don't tell! Makes about 20 fritters, and cheap too! Using the same recipe, add cinnamon, brown sugar and sliced, peeled apples (cut ¼- to ⅜-inch slices) and leave out clams and juice. Makes great apple fritters.

Old Depression Joke. CHILD: "Mama, the garbage man is here." MAMA: "Tell him to leave two cans today, dear."

Mussels Marinière

2	qt mussels	2	sprigs parsley
1	cup dry white wine	1	sprig thyme
2	TB chopped shallot	½	bay leaf
5	TB butter	6	peppercorns

This is a dish made all over the world and I am always surprised at the number of people that won't eat it. Every beach has millions of free mussels. Oh well.

In a large buttered saucepan, put two tablespoons of chopped shallots, a sprig of parsley, a sprig of thyme and ½ bay leaf. Brush and scrape the mussels clean. Make sure that they are tightly closed. (Open ones are sick or dead.) Rinse thoroughly in cold water. Stir so that the shells stay closed (to keep the meat inside). Put in saucepan, add 2 tablespoons of butter in very small pieces, peppercorns and one cup of dry white wine. Cook covered over a high flame. As soon as mussels open they are done: 4 to 6 minutes. Drain, put in a warm bowl and keep hot. Strain rest of stock into a saucepan, removing parsley, thyme and bay leaf. Add three tablespoons of butter to stock, bring to quick boil and pour over mussels. Sprinkle with chopped parsley. Serve with French bread and chilled dry white wine. Don't forget to soak up the sauce.

Grilled Mussels

Prepare as above. Take mussels out of shells, wrap in piece of bacon, thread onto skewer, broil quickly on both sides and serve over rice with a green salad.

Meats

Basic Steak

2 *lb steak*   4 *potatoes (big ones)*

You're living high off the hog when you can eat steak—treasure the moment. It's pretty hard to keep a steak supper under two bucks, so what the hell, splurge every now and again and go for a nice big juicy sirloin, T-bone or porterhouse. If you want to maintain the discipline of the spartan garret, however, buy chuck. The baked potatoes help take up the slack of a half-pound portion of chuck. Trim the fat off your hunk of meat first, then rub in salt, pepper, MSG and maybe a dash of garlic, if you like. Bake the potatoes first, then stick the steak under the broiler (medium hot) for 5 minutes, turn the other side up for 5 minutes, then pull it out and cut through with a knife to see if it's done enough to your taste. DON'T OVERCOOK IT! Let it run a little red, man, and it'll bring out the tiger in your chick. Salad and wine will help her along the road too. Which won't exactly make you feel lousy either.

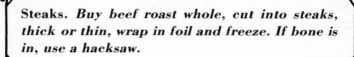

Steaks. *Buy beef roast whole, cut into steaks, thick or thin, wrap in foil and freeze. If bone is in, use a hacksaw.*

Swiss Steak

1	*lb steak*
¼	*cup all-purpose flour*
1	*1-lb can stewed tomatoes*
1	*small can sliced mushrooms*
	meat tenderizer
	pepper

Cut steak into bite-size pieces and tenderize. Mix flour and a small amount of pepper, and coat meat thoroughly. Brown meat in oil in a dutch oven. Add tomatoes and mushrooms, and simmer, covered, over low heat for two hours, or until meat is tender to the fork. This is perfect with mashed potatoes, for the gravy is just fabulous.

Tough Steaks. *To make tough steaks tender and larger, use a hammer. Don't laugh, I do it all the time. Great for horsemeat too!*

Pepper Steak

1½	lb chuck steak		dash of salt
1	TB black pepper	½	cup red wine

This is not the kind of pepper steak that takes the green veg to spice it up—this comes out real hot, so be careful. Rub the black pepper into both sides of the steak and let sit for 30 minutes. Put a little oil in a heavy iron fry pan and heat well. Then cook steak on each side, salting a bit, until done. Remove the steak and pour the wine in the fry pan. Stir it about for one minute. Pour over steak and eat. This goes well with any kind of potato and a salad plus the rest of the wine.

Steak Gravy. *Put a little water in a pan, place under the steak when broiling it on rack. Will make its own gravy. Prevents grease from burning and will eliminate smoke and fire. Put a little foil between pan and rack, and cleaning is a cinch.*

New England Boiled Dinner

1   *lb beef (boiling or stewing)*
    potatoes, peeled
6   *carrots, whole*
6   *onions*
1   *small cabbage, quartered*
    salt and pepper
1   *can tomatoes*

This all-purpose dinner gives you meat, vegetables and salad (and a soup for tomorrow) so inexpensively that you won't believe it until you buy the ingredients and try it for yourself. Cut the beef into 4 equal pieces and throw into a big pot filled with 1½ quarts of water, bring to a boil and then cook over low heat for 30 minutes. Add the potatoes, carrots, onions and 3 of the cabbage quarters plus salt and pepper. Continue cooking for another 20 to 30 minutes, or until vegetables are done. Use the fourth cabbage quarter to make cole slaw (see page 98). Serve dinner, reserving two each of the potatoes, carrots and onions and one of the cabbage quarters. After dinner chop these up and throw back into the pot along with the contents of the can of tomatoes. Simmer for 15 to 20 minutes, let cool and then store in the refrigerator for tomorrow.

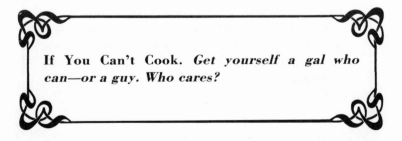

If You Can't Cook. *Get yourself a gal who can—or a guy. Who cares?*

Braised Steak and Potato Dinner

1   *lb boneless chuck steak*
4   *potatoes, peeled and cut in 1" slices*
2   *green peppers, coarsely chopped*
1   *can tomatoes*
    salt and pepper
    flour

This is another basic meat and potato dinner that's tasty, cheap and quick to fix. Flour the steak and brown on both sides in a little oil. Add the tomatoes, cover and simmer for 40 minutes. (Check it once or twice, for you may have to add a bit of water.) Push the steak to one side of the fry pan, add the potatoes, cover and simmer 15 minutes more. Then add peppers, salt and pepper, and simmer for an additional 10 minutes.

Beef Stew

1   *lb stewing beef, cut up*
4   *potatoes, peeled and halved*
4   *carrots, quartered*
4   *small onions, peeled and whole*
1   *small can green peas*
1   *can tomatoes*
½   *tsp oregano*
    salt and pepper
    flour

First brown the meat. Then put it in the stewpot, cover the meat with about an inch of water and simmer for an hour. Add everything else except the peas and tomatoes and simmer another half hour or until the vegetables are done (add water if necessary), then stir in the peas and tomatoes. If you want, thicken the liquid with flour. Stew is best if you age it for a day in the fridge, and serve with hot biscuits.

Baked Pork Chops with Stuffing

4   *pork chops*
   cups stuffing (see p. 53)

With this recipe you can kill two birds with one stone by baking a couple of potatoes along with the chops. First brown the chops in a fry pan. Then put the chops in a casserole with a mound (about ice cream cone scoop size) of stuffing on each chop. Add about ½ inch of water and bake covered at 350° for about 45 minutes. Take the cover off the casserole for the last 15 minutes so the stuffing will brown.

To Make Tough Meat Tender. *Soak it for a few minutes in strong vinegar water.*
To Make Vinegar Water. *Add vinegar to water.*

Tongue Creole

1 lb cooked tongue
1 onion, chopped
1 green pepper, chopped
1 can tomatoes
1 tsp sugar
1 tsp paprika
   salt and pepper
   garlic salt (optional)

This tasty bit of tongue will be appreciated in any language. Gently sauté the pepper and onion seasoned with garlic salt. Then add the tomatoes, sugar and other seasonings and mix well. Place the tongue in a casserole and cover with the other stuff. Bake at 350° for ½ hour, or until tender.

Deep Freezes. *If you can afford a deep freeze you don't need this book. But as long as you've bought it, try cooking with it. It could be quite an experience.*

Cold Tongue

1	*lb tongue*	2	*tsp salt*
4	*cloves*	⅛	*tsp pepper*
4	*peppercorns*	1	*TB vinegar*

When you bite this tongue it won't hurt a bit. Dump everything into a large pot containing at least 2 quarts of water. Bring to a boil and then simmer until tender, usually 3 to 4 hours. Check it now and again, for you may have to add more water. When done, skin the tongue and remove roots. Chill, slice and serve with a tart cocktail sauce or horseradish.

Braised Kidneys

2	*veal kidneys*	1	*TB flour*
1	*small onion, finely chopped*	½	*cup cooking wine*
½	*cup chicken stock or bouillon*	1	*tomato, peeled and chopped*

Kidneys are cheap but kind of hard to find. Try an old-fashioned butcher shop. Sauté kidneys in oil in a fry pan for about five minutes, browning both sides. Add onions and sauté. Then stir in flour, stirring for one minute. Add cooking wine and the stock or bouillon, tomato pieces, salt, pepper and dry mustard. Cover the fry pan and simmer for 15 to 20 minutes, stirring occasionally. Serve with rice.

Kidney Casserole

1	*beef kidney*
6	*carrots, whole or cut up*

3	TB flour	3	tsp salt
¼	cup oil or shortening	¼	tsp pepper
1½	cups beef stock or bouillon		bread crumbs

Once you've transplanted these kidneys into your stomach, you'll never be the same again. Soak kidneys in salt water for ½ hour, remove and simmer in unsalted water for 20 minutes. Then cook in yet another pot of fresh, unsalted water for an hour, or until tender. Brown the flour by baking in a hot oven for a few minutes, then make a sauce by cooking the oil, flour, stock, salt and pepper. Cut the kidneys into small pieces and mix together with sauce and carrots. Put in a greased casserole with buttered bread crumbs on top and bake at 325° until mixture is hot, about 15 to 20 minutes.

Stuffed Heart

| 1 | pork or veal heart |
| 2 | cups stuffing (see p. 53) |

Cheap and different, and the stuffing makes it a great substitute for the Thanksgiving bird or the Christmas goose if you can't afford those traditionals. To cook it, remove veins and arteries from heart and wash. Cover with water, bring to a boil, then simmer for an hour. Drain and stuff and place in a baking dish, adding the heart stock to ½ the depth of the meat. Bake covered at 325°, or until tender. If you like, vegetables such as whole onions, carrots and celery may be added for the last 30 minutes of cooking.

Liver and Bacon

| ½ | lb liver | 8 | slices bacon |

salt and pepper   *flour*

This won't put lead in your pencil, but it's a good source of iron and another one of those "quickie" meals. Pan fry the bacon first. Season the liver with salt and pepper and dredge with flour. Fry the liver in the bacon fat, but do not overcook—3 to 5 minutes on either side is sufficient.

Barbecued Spareribs

2   *lb spare ribs*
    chuckwagon barbecue sauce (see p. 91)

If you think the Colonel's chicken is finger-lickin' good, wait'll you taste these ribs, man. Simmer the ribs in a small amount of water until tender. Place the ribs in a single layer in a shallow baking pan and pour the barbecue sauce over them. Bake at 350° until brown, basting occasionally. If you want your ribs "Yankee style," you can stuff them with stuffing (see page 53) or bake the stuffing in a separate baking dish.

Gretchen's Goulash

1-1½   *lb stewing beef*   *noodles*

This old Mormon dish came into vogue when the wives and kids began to outdistance the old man's pocketbook. Gretchen, legend has it, was the 23rd and last of one of the Latter Day Beard's wives, who was so adept at her nocturnal cooking chores that the bearded one gave a name to her only legitimate culinary effort.

Well, to begin this Mormon mishmash, cut the beef into bite-size chunks and brown in some butter or oil in the fry pan. Then turn the flame down low, salt and pepper it, add lots of paprika and a couple of cups of water, and cover and simmer about a half hour. Stir occasionally so you'll wind up with a thickish red paprika-beef sauce. Serve over buttered noodles sprinkled with caraway seeds.

Grilled Franks

8   *franks*   8   *strips bacon*
2   *TB mustard*   1   *green sweet pepper*
8   *strips cheese*

Score franks lengthwise. Spread with mustard and insert a strip of cheese and green pepper. Twist bacon around franks and secure with a toothpick. Fry in moderate hot fat, or grill. Serve with boiled or mashed potatoes and mustard. Also good with beans and ketch-up.

Hot Dogs. *Take a moment and try this. Slit hot dogs lengthwise but not through. Place piece of cheese (sharp cheddar) with a little hot mustard in the slit. Wrap with bacon and pin with toothpicks at ends. Fry or broil. Very nice. Break off toothpicks if too long.*

Beef in Wine Sauce

1 *lb chuck steak, cubed*
1 *small can mushroom bits*
1 *can peas*

2 *onions, chopped*
1 *cup red wine*
2 *cups water*

This is a fine gourmet meal with a French name that we have forgotten. Brown the steak in oil in a heavy iron fry pan. Add the wine and water and the rest of the stuff. Season with tarragon and a bay leaf. Cook slowly until meat is tender, stirring on occasion. You may have to add a dab more water, or wine if you prefer. This is great with a salad, a bit of cheese for dessert and the leftover wine to wash it down with.

Barbecue Sauce

1 *small can tomato sauce*
¼ *cup vinegar*
2 *tsp dry mustard*
¼ *tsp black pepper*
½ *tsp salt*
2 *beef bouillon cubes*
1 *TB butter or marge*
½ *tsp Worcestershire sauce*
½ *tsp sugar*

This is not only an addition to whatever you've barbecued, but it's right tasty on hamburgers, steak, chicken or whatever. To make it, merely combine all ingredients and simmer for 10 minutes, stirring it about once in a while.

Duck Glaze

¼   *cup honey*
½   *tsp Kitchen Bouquet*
½   *tsp salt*
½   *tsp powdered ginger*

This will not only sweeten up your duck, but it also enhances ham or yams as well. All you have to do is mix it well and then brush it on whatever you want glazed.

Meatless Tuesdays

Simple Spaghetti

1	*medium can tomato sauce*	1	*clove of garlic*
1	*lb spaghetti, #9*	½	*stick butter*
1	*onion, large*		*pinch of rosemary*

Brown onion and garlic in oil, add the can of sauce and pinch of rosemary, and allow to simmer over low heat. Put spaghetti in boiling water for 8 minutes, strain and put aside. Put ½ stick of butter in same pot, add

spaghetti and a little sauce. Stir with heat on for about 3 minutes (total cooking time about 11 minutes). Serve on a heated platter, putting the remaining sauce on top. Use a little grated cheese if you have some. Pretty good and pretty cheap.

"Fat" Spaghetti

1	*lb ziti*	1	*onion, chopped*
1	*green pepper, chopped*	1	*can tomato soup*

For those who don't speak Italian, ziti is 1" long pieces of macaroni and, therefore, those of you who are too dense to realize where "fat" comes from, think about it. Anyway, sauté the peppers and onion in a bit of oil while cooking the ziti in a separate pot. When the peppers and onion are soft, stir in the can of soup, add salt, pepper, garlic salt and a dash of oregano. When the "fat" spaghetti is done (about 10 minutes), drain and stir in the rest of the guck. Serve with meatballs, hamburgers or whatever.

Macaroni and Cheese

1	*box macaroni*
¼-½	*lb American cheese*
1	*qt milk*

Boil from a ½ pound to 1 pound of macaroni in a couple of quarts of salted water for 10 minutes and then drain. Cut up the cheese (save a few pieces) and dump into a saucepan containing two cups of milk. Heat gently (do not boil) until the cheese dissolves. Thicken the cheese sauce with cornstarch and mix with the macaroni. Dump the whole works into a greased casserole dish, add a little more milk to make it moist, put on the top the pieces of cheese you saved, and pop into the oven (325°) for 10 to 15 minutes.

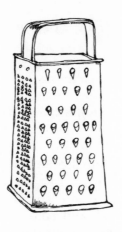

Vegetable Loaf

1	*eggplant, peeled and diced*	½	*cup dried bread crumbs*
1	*cup diced celery*	4	*TB butter*
1	*onion, chopped*	½	*tsp oregano*
1	*tomato, diced*		*garlic powder*
1	*egg*		*salt*

This is a quickie if you're a real Meatless Tuesday buff. Sauté all the vegetables in butter for 3 or 4 minutes. Let it cool and put in a mixing bowl, adding the bread crumbs, egg, oregano and garlic powder, and salt to taste. Mix well. Place in a greased, 8-inch baking pan or casserole, and bake for 25 minutes in a 350° oven.

McSorley's Old Ale House Mustard

½   *cup dry mustard*   *McSorley's ale*

If you're still buying prepared mustard at today's prices, shame on you. We haven't bought any in years. Try our old McSorley's wonderful saloon recipe. (Still our favorite spot despite the new rules liberating the joint.) Weekends are college nights, and beware on St. Paddy's day.

Buy mustard in powdered form in 1-lb cans—the type that restaurants use. Comes light, brown, golden, hot or cold. We use Endeco, distributed by Louis Ender, Inc., NYC. Hot! Thing to remember about mustard is, never add fresh mustard to old, and cover and refrigerate when not in use. Mix dry mustard with McSorley's ale to the consistency of thick cream. Let age 20 minutes to develop its flavor. Caution, use sparingly till accustomed. Grows on one.

If you can't get McSorley's ale, use any ale. If no ale, use beer. If no beer, you've got a problem.

Actually, mustard will mix well with all of the following, and more: water, stale beer, wine, sugar, cider, vinegar, molasses, black pepper, cayenne pepper and salt, and is generally named after any main ingredient or a country. Mint, orange (use the grated rind of lime or lemon), horseradish, curry, garlic (this will flip you), chili, celery seed, etc. Have fun. In general one teaspoon of any main ingredient to one cup of dry mustard.

Soups

Old-fashioned Vegetable Soup

1	soup bone	¼-½	head cabbage
4	potatoes	1	can tomato sauce
2	carrots		bay leaf
1	onion		

Good for at least two or three days' eating. The bone is the heart of it, a good beef bone from the local butcher. You can probably con him out of it for nothing. If not, he won't charge you more than 15 cents. The other items figure to around a nickel or a dime each. Fill the big pot with cold water, and drop in the bone and a bit of salt and boil off about a third of the water—about two hours. Add the tomato sauce and the vegetables (cut

Port Wine. *A little added to homemade tomato soup does something for the flavor. Adds zip.*

small) and a bay leaf and simmer for a couple more hours. Season with imagination. Tastes better if you let it stand a day before eating.

Cuban Black Bean Soup

2	*cans (16 oz) black beans*	¼	*tsp oregano*
1	*large onion, chopped*	1	*TB sherry*
⅓	*cup olive oil*	¼	*tsp sugar*
2	*pimentos, chopped*		*pinch of salt*

Sauté onion and pimentos in oil. Add remaining ingredients, including the liquid from the beans, and simmer 5 minutes. Can be served over rice as well.

Starving Artist Bean Soup

1	*pork shoulder bone*	1	*turnip*
1	*stalk celery*	1	*parsnip*
1	*onion*		*pinch of salt*
1	*carrot*	4-5	*bay leaves*

½	cup dried beans	1	cup large lima beans
	(red, white and black)		sage
¼	cup dried peas		rosemary
	(yellow and green)		thyme
1	large can tomatoes		pepper

The next time you are at one of your friend's for dinner, scrounge the leftover pork shoulder bone. Make sure they leave a little meat and fat on it. Rough cut all the vegetables and the meat and the fat, and boil together with 4 to 5 bay leaves in 4 quarts of water for 20 minutes. Add ½ cup of each of the beans, red, white and black. Add a little split-pea beans, yellow and green, 1 large can of tomatoes, and cook slowly till done, about 3 hours covered. Stir about every ½ hour, and add the lima beans about ½ hour before soup is done, along with lots of thyme and a pinch of rosemary and sage. Serve with homemade corn bread. A meal for eight starving artists, one of whom should be able to afford the wine.

Put the leftover in plastic jars and freeze. Renew before using again by adding a little ketchup and a glass of red wine. Managed well, this dish can last from about six months to a year!

Split Pea Soup

½	lb dry green split peas
2	onions, chopped
2	large carrots cut in ½-inch lengths
1	clove of garlic, finely chopped
1	tsp salt
1	tsp sugar
	dash of black pepper

One of the nicest things about this soup is that it

has such a lovely color and it's so simple to make. Bring two quarts of water to the boil. Add all the ingredients, turn down the heat, and let it simmer for 45 minutes. Toward the end, stir occasionally, checking the peas for softness. When they are completely soft but not yet pureed (real mushy), your soup is did. Now *eat.*

Mushroom and Potato Soup

6   *¼-inch strips salt pork*
4   *medium potatoes*
2   *15½-oz cans mushrooms (bits and pieces)*
    flour
2   *onions*

This is a dandy, a quick soup to start off any meal or to stand up all by itself at mealtime. Peel and thinly slice the potatoes, throw in a 2-quart pot of water and bring to a boil. Render the fat from the salt pork in a fry pan and toss the pork in the pot with the spuds. Coarsely chop onions and brown in fat. When brown, sprinkle with ⅓ cup flour, and when flour is brown, add enough liquid from pot to make a thin paste. When potatoes are tender to a fork, throw the paste in the pot

Depression Chicken Soup. *Put a two-quart pot of water on the stove. Add a little salt. When the water comes to a boil, run a chicken through the kitchen.*

along with the mushrooms (including juice) and simmer for about 10 minutes. Season to taste with salt and pepper.

Black-eyed Pea Soup

1   *large can black-eyed peas with pork*
3   *cups beef bouillon (use 3 cubes dissolved in boiling water)*
1   *large onion, chopped*
1   *tsp Worcestershire sauce*
2   *TB bacon fat*

You can use two cups of dried peas if you want, but it takes tremendously longer. This is real nourishing and can stand by itself for lunch, particularly if you put some hot corn bread and a glass of milk alongside it. Gently sauté the onion in the fat until light brown. Add the rest of the stuff, salt and pepper to taste, and cook over a low flame for 15 minutes.

Iron Utensils. *Wash in hot sudsy water with washing soda. Dry, coat with bacon grease, wrap in plastic tissue and store in a dry place. A good old one is a rare item these days, and brother, will they cook!*

Chicken Vegetable Soup

½   *lb chicken wings, backs or necks*
2   *large potatoes, peeled and cubed*
1   *large onion, chopped*
1   *small can peas and carrots*
1   *handful of rice*
     salt and pepper

This brand of Jewish penicillin will not only cure whatever ails you but will put some meat on your bones to boot. Bring a quart and a half of water to boil and throw in the bird. Turn the heat to low and cook, covered, for ½ hour, or until chicken is tender. Take the pieces of chicken out of the pot and set aside to cool. Put everything else in the pot except the peas and carrots, and cook ½ hour more on low heat. Then throw in the peas and carrots and the chicken meat that has been stripped from the bone, and simmer ½ hour longer.

Clam Chowder

2   *slices bacon, cut up*   1   *10-oz can clams*
1   *onion, chopped*   1   *cup milk*
2   *stalks celery, chopped*   1   *qt water*
3   *potatoes, cut up*   ½   *tsp oregano*
3   *carrots, cut up*   *salt and pepper*

This chowder ends up so thick it's practically a three-course dinner. First, sauté the bacon, onion and celery, and set aside. In a large pot, slowly cook the potatoes and carrots in the quart of water. When nearly done, add the clams (including liquid) and the seasonings, and simmer for 10 minutes. Add the bacon, onions and celery, and simmer 10 minutes more. Take off the fire and stir in the milk. Reheat, but do not bring to a boil before serving. For Manhattan style clam chowder, add a small can of tomato sauce when you add the clams.

Corn Chowder

1 *can whole kernel corn, drained*
1 *small onion, thinly sliced*
2 *large potatoes, cut up in small chunks*
3 *cups milk*
 salt and pepper

This is a very easy and quick soup (chowder) to make. Gently sauté the onion in a saucepan. Add the corn and potatoes and enough boiling water to cover to a depth of 1 inch. Cook until tender, about 10 to 15 minutes. Add milk and salt and pepper. Stir and simmer for another 5 minutes.

Chicken Gumbo Soup

3 *cups chicken stock*
1 *cup cooked chicken, cut up small*

Formal Lunch. *In giving a formal lunch it is of the utmost importance to select the right combinations of food and to have enough courses—but not too many.*

1   *small can tomatoes*
1   *onion, chopped*
1   *green pepper, chopped*
1   *small can okra, drained*
1   *handful of rice*
    salt and pepper

This isn't exactly New Orleans style, but even a dyed-in-the-wool Cajun will admit it runs a close second. If you don't have chicken stock, make it by using chicken bouillon and water. Sauté the onion until soft. Throw everything else into the soup pot and bring to a boil and immediately turn heat to very low and simmer for 15 to 20 minutes. Stir occasionally. If you don't have or can't afford the chicken, leave it out, for it's still a good soup. And if you're in the bucks, you can throw in a small can of cooked shrimp or crab meat or both. If you do, of course, you'll have to change the name of the gumbo.

Potato Soup à la Cress

1   *lb potatoes, peeled*
1   *bunch watercress, chopped*
1   *TB butter*
½   *cup milk*
     salt and pepper

This is just about one of the cheapest, and tastiest, soups you can make. Boil the spuds until very well done, but not too mushy. Into 4 cups of the potato water, add the potatoes after running them through a sieve. Add chopped watercress and cook, stirring occasionally, for 5 minutes. Add butter, milk and salt and pepper and simmer for 10 minutes more.

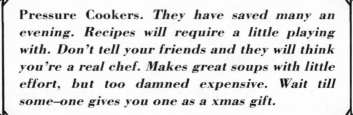

> Pressure Cookers. *They have saved many an evening. Recipes will require a little playing with. Don't tell your friends and they will think you're a real chef. Makes great soups with little effort, but too damned expensive. Wait till some–one gives you one as a xmas gift.*

Lima Bean Soup

⅓   *lb dried lima beans*
⅛   *lb salt pork, cut up*
     or
4   *slices bacon, cut up*
1   *large onion, chopped*
1   *small can tomato sauce (optional)*
    salt and pepper

Like anything else made from beans, this will make you go "poop" a little bit, so be sure to warn your dining companion. Pick and wash the beans. Dump everything into a pot containing 1½ quarts of water, except for the tomato sauce, and bring to a boil. Turn the heat to low and cook for one hour. Turn heat down to simmer and add tomato sauce, and cook for another half hour, stirring now and again.

Yankee Bean Soup

The ingredients and method of making this are exactly the same as that of lima bean soup. The only

To Clean Iron Sinks. *Rub them well with a cloth wet with kerosene oil.*

Stews, soups and chili should be aged for a day in the refrigerator before serving.

difference is that there is an increase in the tendency to afflatus. Why this should be no one knows. But there we are.

Borscht

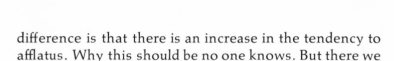

6	*large beets, peeled and finely shredded*
6	*cups beef bouillon stock*
1	*TB vinegar*
¼	*tsp sugar*
	salt and pepper

You can serve this Red Russian soup either hot or cold, but cold is better. Cover the shredded beets with the stock, and cook until the beets are soft. Add the rest of the stuff and simmer for another 30 minutes.

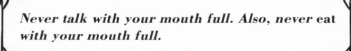

Never talk with your mouth full. Also, never eat with your mouth full.

Food with Soul

Chicken Wing Stew

1	*lb chicken wings*	1	*small can peas*
4	*large potatoes*	1	*can mushroom soup*
1	*onion, chopped*		

Peel and halve the spuds, and cook with wings in 2 quarts of water for about 20 minutes. Lower the flame, add the onions, peas and mushroom soup, and stir well. Salt and pepper gently and simmer for 30 minutes. This is a good place to use dumplings (page 106). For trimmings serve hot biscuits and salad.

Black-eyed Peas

⅓ *lb black-eyes (dry)*   4 *slices bacon*
⅛ *lb salt pork*   *salt and pepper*
  or

Black-eyes are not only nutritious but, as the legend goes, if you eat them on New Year's Day they'll bring you luck for the rest of the year. The luck will be either good or bad, although sometimes it's the reverse.

Wash and pick the peas first. Cut up the salt pork or bacon, and throw in a saucepan along with the peas. Cover the peas with 2 inches of cold water, add salt and pepper and then bring to a boil. Bring the heat to very low and cook covered for an hour, or until tender. Stir occasionally, and you may have to add a dab or two of water.

Southern Style Green Beans

1 *lb fresh green beans*
¼ *lb bacon or bacon ends*
1 *onion, chopped*

You can't get this kind of green bean out of a can. Cut up the bacon into inch-long pieces. Wash the beans and cut off the ends. Cook the bacon slowly in the bottom of a saucepan until you have a coating of bacon grease on the bottom of the pot. Add the onions, then the beans. Cover and cook over a low, low flame for about 20 minutes. Then stir about a bit and check beans for doneness. You may have to cook a bit longer, but don't overcook.

Cheese-fried Grits

1   *cup white grits*
5   *cups water*
1   *egg*
1   *cup grated sharp cheese*
    salt
    dash of cayenne pepper

This bit of soul food takes time, but it's lip-smacking good. Slowly add grits to boiling water, add salt and pepper and cook slowly for 20 to 30 minutes. Let it cool, add the cheese, mold into croquettes and refrigerate several hours or let stand overnight. Dip the croquettes in the beaten egg and fry, preferably in bacon or ham fat. These can also be made into patties if you don't know what a croquette is.

Yellow Turnips

1   *large yellow turnip*
2   *slices salt pork*
1   *TB brown sugar*
½   *cup bread crumbs*
½   *tsp crushed red pepper*

More soul food. Peel and cube turnip. Render fat

from salt pork. Throw away the pork and cook turnips, seasoned with red pepper, in enough water to cover. Cook for about 20 minutes, or until done. Put cooked turnips in a greased baking dish, cover with the mixed bread crumbs and sugar and bake at 350° for 10 minutes.

Salt Will Curdle New Milk. *Therefore, in preparing porridge, gravies, etc., the salt should not be added until the dish is prepared.*

Texas Type Cooking

Salt Steak

1½ *lb chuck steak*
2   *cups salt*

Grill this steak in a coat of salt. Crack off the coat, then lay some bread on your plate to soak up all the juice. Texas, here I come! Sprinkle both sides of steak with pepper and garlic powder and rub in. Mix the salt with enough water to make a thick paste. Put half the salt paste on one side of steak and broil salt side up for about 15 minutes in the oven. Remove the salt, turn steak over and repeat process. To serve, remove remaining salt crust, and cover steak with Lone Star Steak Sauce. Serve this with home fried potatoes and biscuits.

Chicken Fried Steak

1	*lb ½-inch-thick round steak*	1½	*tsp salt*
⅓	*cup flour*	½	*tsp pepper*

They used to call this "prairie chicken" when they was eating off a chuck wagon. Cut the steak into two pieces. Mix the flour, salt and pepper, and sprinkle over both sides of the steak, pounding it in well. Fry steak for five minutes on both sides in at least ½ cup oil or shortening. Mashed potatoes, green beans and pan gravy make this a sumptuous meal.

Lone Star Steak Sauce

¼	*lb butter*	½	*tsp black pepper*
⅓	*cup lemon juice*	½	*tsp dry mustard*
2	*TB Worcestershire sauce*		*dash of tabasco*
1	*clove garlic, minced*		*dash of salt*

This sauce is so good it'll bring out the flavor even in old Wily Coyote. Mix it all together in a bowl and beat until the butter melts. You can add the broiler pan juice to it if you want. Serve it over salt steak. It'll even make a Damn Yankee–cooked steak edible. *Man.*

Chuckwagon Barbecue Sauce

1	*cup strong black coffee*
1½	*cup Worcestershire sauce*

1 cup ketchup	2 TB sugar
¼ lb butter	1 TB salt
¼ cup lemon juice	2 tsp cayenne pepper

Combine all ingredients and simmer for 30 minutes over a low flame. Beef, ribs, chicken or just plain old steak take on a new flavor.

Cowboy Beans

½ lb dried pinto beans
2 cups cold water
¼ lb salt pork, cut up
1 onion, chopped
1 clove garlic, minced
1 small can tomato paste
1½ TB chili powder
1 tsp salt
½ tsp cayenne pepper

Serve these with corn bread or chili, or if you have some leftover, refry them. Wash the beans and then soak them in water overnight. Next morning put beans and water in a large pot and bring to a boil. Cover, reduce the fire, simmer for an hour. Stir in the rest of the stuff and simmer, covered, for 2½ to 3 hours more, or until tender. Check occasionally, for you may have to add a little more water.

Texas "Red" Chili

1½ lb round steak, cut into bite-size pieces
6 TB chili powder
1 TB oregano

1   *TB crushed cumin seed*
1   *TB salt*
½   *TB cayenne pepper*
2   *cloves garlic, minced*
1   *TB tabasco (beware, this is HOT!)*
1½ *qt water*
½   *cup white cornmeal*

This dates back to the streets of San Antone in the 1800s, long before they had ice cream or hot dog vendors. In a Dutch oven or other big pot, brown the meat in a little cooking oil. Add the rest of the stuff except the cornmeal and bring to a boil. Reduce the heat and simmer covered for 1½ hours. Stir in the cornmeal and simmer, uncovered, for another 30 minutes, stirring occasionally. Serve with red beans or rice and corn bread.

Sourdough Starter

1   *pkg dry yeast*   2   *cups all-purpose flour*
2   *cups warm water*   1   *TB sugar*

The goldminers up in the Yukon and the chuck wagon cooks in the Southwest made sourdough famous, but it was used for making biscuits and bread and flapjacks long before their time. Use a wide-mouthed glass jar, or a crock, to mix and store the sourdough in. First soften and dissolve the yeast in the warm water. Add the sugar, then stir in the flour and mix well. Cover with cheesecloth, paper towel or foil, and fasten around the mouth of the jar with a rubber band. Poke a couple of holes in this cover so the dough can breathe. Let it age for about 24 hours in a warm place, then store it in the refrigerator. After using some of the starter, replace with an equal amount of both water and flour. (For instance, if you use one cup of starter, replace with one cup of water and one cup of flour.)

Sourdough Biscuits

1   *cup all-purpose flour*
1   *tsp sugar*
2   *tsp baking powder*
½   *tsp salt*
1   *cup sourdough starter*
2   *TB lard or shortening*

A couple of these biscuits would make the grumpiest old cowpoke offer to go cut firewood for the cook. They go good with anything and make a fine base for strawberry shortcake. Mix the flour, salt, sugar and baking powder in a large bowl. Cut in the lard and pour in the starter. Mix to a firm dough. On a floured surface, pat the dough out to a thick, 9-inch circle. Cut out biscuits with a water glass and put in a greased baking tin or pie plate. Let rise for 10 or 15 minutes and then bake in a 350° oven for 15 to 25 minutes.

Sourdough Bread

5   *cups all-purpose flour*
1½ *cups sourdough starter*
1   *pkg dry yeast*
⅓   *cup sugar*
⅓   *cup shortening*
2   *TB lukewarm water*
1   *cup milk*
1   *tsp salt*

This is just good old plain bread with no phony stuff in it. It makes two loaves and should last you for at least a week, for about 20 cents a loaf. Scald the milk and add the sugar, salt and shortening, stirring to melt sugar and shortening. Dissolve the yeast in lukewarm water. Then beat together the cooled milk mixture, yeast, sourdough starter and two cups of flour. Then add the remaining flour, a bit at a time, to make a stiff dough. Turn out on a floured surface and knead for 10 minutes. Lightly grease (butter or shortening) all sides of the dough and place in a greased bowl. Let rise until it doubles in size, about 1½ hours. Punch it down and let rise for another ½ hour. Cut the dough into two balls, shape into loaves and put each loaf in a greased, 9-inch bread pan. Let rise for one more hour. Bake in a 400° oven for about 40 minutes.

Sourdough Corn Bread

1½	cups cornmeal
1½	TB sugar
1½	tsp salt
1½	cups milk
1½	cups sourdough starter
1½	tsp cream of tartar (optional)
1½	tsp baking soda
2	eggs, beaten
6	TB melted butter

Hot buttered corn bread, a plate of beans and a couple of cups of coffee used to be part of the cowboy's standard diet. It's still a good meal. Combine the cornmeal, sugar and salt in a mixing bowl. Scald the milk, pour over cornmeal and cool to lukewarm. Add the rest of the ingredients and mix well. Pour into a greased 9-inch baking tin and bake in a 450° oven for 40 minutes.

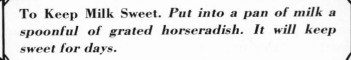

To Keep Milk Sweet. *Put into a pan of milk a spoonful of grated horseradish. It will keep sweet for days.*

Sourdough Flapjacks

2½	cups all-purpose flour
1	cup sourdough starter
2	eggs, beaten
2	cups lukewarm water
⅓	cup half and half (condensed milk will do)
1	TB baking soda
2	TB sugar
2	TB cooking oil

For best results, mix flour, water and sourdough starter in a bowl and keep overnight in the icebox. Stir in the remaining ingredients (including the oil) and let bubble for about 10 minutes. Cook on a griddle or iron fry pan like regular pancakes. If you have some batter left over, it will keep for a day or so.

Salads

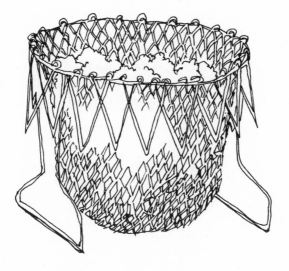

Lettuce and Tomato Salad

1 *head lettuce*
2 *large tomatoes*

This is the basic salad and easiest to whip up, and costs from 20 to 30 cents, depending on the season.

Simplest dressing is vinegar and oil. Several ways to serve it up. Quarter the lettuce and slice the tomatoes. Quarter the tomato slices, shred the lettuce and mix. Peel off big leaves of lettuce and garnish with slices of tomato. No matter how you serve it it tastes refreshing and is nourishing.

Cucumber and Tomato Salad

1   *cucumber, peeled and sliced*
2   *tomatoes, sliced*
2   *or 3 lettuce leaves*

Another quick and easy salad. Arrange the cucumbers and tomatoes on the lettuce and top with the dressing of your choice. There are many variations you can try: add deviled eggs, carrot sticks, shallots, radishes, olives, celery stalks, cottage cheese or any combination of these.

Cole Slaw with Vinegar Dressing

3   *cups shredded cabbage*
¼   *cup green pepper, finely diced*
3   *oz white vinegar*
½   *cup salad oil*
1½   *oz water*
¼   *tsp salt*
1   *TB sugar*

Cole Slaw with Mayonnaise Dressing

4   *cups shredded cabbage*
1½   *cups mayonnaise*

Picnic Lunches. *The question of what to eat at a picnic meal depends entirely on where the picnic is to be given.*

1   TB Worcestershire sauce
2   TB ketchup

Cole slaw is one of the easiest and quickest salads to make. Also, cabbage is cheap and healthy, and all the ingredients should be on stock in your cupboard or icebox. To make, simply mix all the dressings (either vinegar or mayonnaise types) together, pour over the cabbage and toss. Be sure to chill before serving.

Watercress Salad

1   *bunch watercress, trimmed, rinsed well and drained*
¼   *cup pimento stuffed olives*
¼   *cup French dressing*

This is one of the best "natural" salads, a little different from the ordinary and mighty tasty. Mix all ingredients and toss gently. Chill for about 20 to 30 minutes before serving.

School Lunches. *Much care and thought should be given to the planning of meals for children.*

Deviled Eggs

4   *hard-boiled eggs, cold*   *salt and pepper*
⅓   *tsp dry mustard*   *mayonnaise*

These may be the work of the Devil, but they taste heavenly. And they're not really a salad, but there's no place else to put them in this Good Book. Remove the shells, cut lengthwise or crosswise through the eggs, and remove the yolks. Mash the yolks, mix with the seasonings and add enough mayo to make smooth. Fill the hollows in the eggs with the paste and garnish each little devil with a dash of paprika.

Potato Salad

6   *boiled potatoes, cold*   2   *TB vinegar*
    and peeled   *milk*
1   *onion, chopped*   *salt and pepper*
1   *hard-boiled egg, cut up*   *paprika*
½   *cup mayonnaise*

Coarsely cut up the spuds as you would for home fries. Add the onion, egg and seasoning, and mix. Thin the mayo with just a little bit of milk, pour over the potatoes and mix once again. Chill before serving.

To Prevent Oil from Becoming Rancid. *Drop a few drops of ether into the bottle containing it.*

Wilted Dandelion Green Salad

1	qt dandelion greens	2	TB vinegar
4	strips bacon, diced	½	tsp salt
2	tsp sugar		dash of black pepper
¼	tsp dry mustard		

When the lowly dandelion begins to come up in the spring, your salad bill goes down. Wash the greens thoroughly and chop coarsely. Fry the bacon until crisp and brown. Add the other ingredients to the grease, and heat and stir until the sugar dissolves. Pour this mixture over the shredded greens and toss with the diced bacon.

Arturo's Squid Salad

1   lb baby squid, cleaned
4   hard-boiled eggs
3   ribs celery, rough cut
1   large onion, rough cut in ¼" square pieces
1   cup red pepper, diced
1   cup green pepper, diced
2   medium sweet pickles, diced
½   tsp dry mustard
¾   cup olive oil
2   cups cider vinegar
1   tsp tarragon
1   TB parsley
    pinch of sugar
    salt and pepper to taste

Put squid in boiling water with a little vinegar and salt added. Boil for 3 minutes, remove and drain. Cut squid into pieces the same size as you cut the tentacles (keep uniform), set aside. Make two cups of vinaigrette sauce by cooking down herbs, oil, vinegar, and mustard to yield about two cups. Add diced sweet pickles and the white of one egg cut up fine. Pour all over squid and add vegetables and the yokes of the eggs, broken up. Cover and marinate in the refrigerator at least 4 days. Correct seasoning by adding oil or vinegar to make tart or bland. Now add rest of eggs chopped up and marinate for 2 more days. Serve on a bed of spinach or lettuce, and decorate with sliced egg, pimento, cucumber and tomato, or serve separately as an hors d'oeuvre. P.S.: Call it a lobster salad!

Proverb. *"To make a good salad just four persons are wanted: a spendthrift to furnish the oil, a miser to measure the vinegar, a counselor to dole out salt and spices, and a madman to toss it."*

Breads

Padde's Pan Bread

6	cups flour	1	TB salt
	package dry yeast	1	tsp sugar
2	cups warm water		

This makes a loaf that even Henry Miller would approve of.* Makes two 1-pound loaves or one big,

*See Henry's essay, *The Staff of Life*.

round, fat one. Costs 15 to 20 cents. Dissolve the yeast in the warm water along with the salt and sugar. Gradually stir in the flour until the dough will absorb no more. Knead on a floured board four or five times only, cover with a towel and let rise in a warm nook for two hours. Cut the dough in two and shape as you will or let it go as one big round loaf. Bake in a greased pan in a hot oven for about 30 minutes. To give it a nice brown, crusty look, butter the top about five minutes before taking out of the oven. Best way to keep any bread when not in use is to store in the refrig in a brown paper sack or plastic bag tightly closed.

Baking Powder Biscuits

2	cups flour	2	TB baking powder
⅓	cup oil	1	tsp salt
⅔	cup milk		

Hot biscuits are the making of any meal, and they only take about 15 minutes to whip up. They cost about a dime. Mix the flour and baking powder and salt together. Cut in the cooking oil (shortening or bacon grease can be used) with a fork, then add the milk, also using the fork to mix it. Put the dough on a floured surface, pat out to a half-inch thickness, and use a beer or highball glass to cut out the biscuits. Place on a

Troublesome Ants. *A heavy chalk mark laid a finger's distance around your sugar box will surely prevent ants from troubling.*

greased baking tin and bake in a hot oven 15 minutes, or until brown on top.

Corn Bread

1	cup all-purpose flour
1	cup cornmeal
1	egg, beaten
1½	cups milk, sour milk or buttermilk
1	tsp salt
2	TB sugar (optional)
2	tsp baking powder
2	TB oil or melted shortening

Combine all the dry ingredients. Stir in the milk, then the egg and then the oil or shortening. Mix well. Bake in greased baking dish at 425° for 30 minutes.

Some persons sit at table in T-shirts—regrettably of both sexes. This is a very vulgar practice. It is best to remove the T-shirt.

Simple Dumplings

2   *cups flour*
3   *tsp baking powder*
1   *tsp salt*
¾   *cup milk*

Mix all dry ingredients and add enough milk (about ¾ of a cup). An egg may be added if desired. Drop batter by large spoonfuls into stew, cook 10 minutes without cover, and then 10 minutes with cover on. Remove and serve immediately.

Foreign Cuisine

Spanish Omelet

2	*medium potatoes, cubed*	6	*eggs*
1	*small onion, diced*		*salt and pepper*

For some reason or other, the Spanish call a regular omelet, made with just eggs, a French omelet. They almost always put spuds in theirs. Sauté onions and potatoes in oil or butter until the potatoes are light brown. Beat the eggs with salt and pepper and pour over the onions and potatoes. Then proceed as in making a regular omelet.

Czech Bread Dumplings

2 *eggs*
½ *cup milk*
3 *cups flour, sifted, with a pinch of baking powder*
4 *slices white bread, cubed*
1 *tsp salt*

This makes probably the world's largest dumpling. Beat eggs, salt and milk in a large mixing bowl, add flour gradually. Continue beating with a large spoon, stirring bread cubes in at the very last. Dough must be smooth and stiff enough to hold its own shape. Have a clean, wet towel ready on the table. With your hands, shape the dough into *one* oblong dumpling. Roll the dumpling in the towel and carefully drop into a large pot of salted, rapidly boiling water. Boil, covered, at high heat for 45 minutes. Gently remove it from the water and take off the towel. Immediately slice into ½-inch-thick slices. (If you don't slice it immediately, the steam can't escape and the dumpling will be soggy and hard.) Serve with almost any meat that has a nice gravy.

Beef with Sour Cream and Dill Sauce (Czechoslovakia)

1½ *lbs boiling beef*
1   *pkg soup greens*
1½ *TB fresh dill, finely chopped*
½   *cup sour cream*
1½ *TB vinegar*

The joy of this recipe is that it also gives you a hearty soup to go along with the meal. Boil the beef with the soup greens and a dash of salt and pepper in about two quarts of water until the beef is tender. Take the beef out and reserve 1½ cups of the stock (strained). Add some noodles or barley to the remaining stock in the pot and simmer until the soup is done. Meanwhile put the 1½ cups of stock you reserved in a saucepan with the dill and vinegar. Bring to a boil, then simmer for ½ hour, then thicken with a bit of flour. Add the sour cream, stirring gently over a low flame until sauce is smooth and creamy. Then put the beef in the sauce and reheat. Serve with the soup and bread dumplings.

Zucchini and Potatoes (Italy)

1	*big zucchini*	1	*onion*
2	*large potatoes*	1	*small can tomato sauce*

This is a cheap Italian side dish that winds up more like a soup than a vegetable combination. Peel the zucchini and potatoes, and dice into 1-inch cubes. Chop the onion and sauté in a saucepan until golden, then add the potatoes, tomato sauce and two tomato sauce cans of water, plus a little salt and pepper, and garlic salt if you like it. Simmer 15 minutes, or until spuds are tender but not soft. Add zucchini, stir about a bit, cover and simmer another 20 minutes.

Refried Beans (Mexico)

1   *15-oz can pinto or red kidney beans*
1   *medium onion, chopped*
1½   *tsp chili powder*
¼   *tsp garlic powder*
     dash of salt and pepper

If you're a dedicated bean eater, this is a new adventure. Mash the beans with a fork or in an electric mixer, if you have one. Stir in the other ingredients. Melt some butter or oil or shortening in a fry pan and cook the beans slowly over a low fire, stirring occasionally, until the beans have thickened. For a super Mexican dinner, serve the beans with some chili con carne, tamales and tortillas, if you can find them. If not, substitute corn bread.

Green Bean Soup (Germany)

1	lb fresh green beans	3	qt water
2	cups cooked ham, diced	1	tsp salt
		1	tsp black pepper
2	large potatoes, diced	½	tsp garlic powder
1	large onion, chopped	3	TB flour
4	strips bacon	1½	cups milk

In a large pot combine the green beans, potatoes, ham, water and the seasonings. Cover and boil gently for about 25 minutes or until potatoes are tender but not mushy. Meanwhile sauté the bacon (cut into bits) with the onion, and also mix the flour and milk together. Add these ingredients to the soup after the potatoes are tender, turn the flame down low, and simmer covered for another 15 minutes.

To Prevent Rust on Flatirons. *Beeswax and salt will make your rusty flatirons as smooth and clean as glass.*

Polish Sauerkraut

1	or 2 lbs pork neck bones	1	carrot
1	can sauerkraut (large)	1	large potato

Pork bones run about 15 cents a pound and sauerkraut 20 cents a can. Place the pork bones in the bottom of the large pot, add the cut-up carrot and potato and the salt and pepper. Throw in the kraut, and add cold water to the level of the cabbage. Bring to a boil, then let simmer softly for about an hour. Stir occasionally. Pork flavor permeates the kraut, and there's a lot of meat on the bones.

Gazpacho (Spain)

4   cups chicken broth or bouillon, chilled
4   tomatoes, diced
1   onion, diced
2   green peppers, diced
1   stalk celery, diced
2   TB olive oil
⅓   cup lemon juice
    dash of tabasco sauce

Chill this Spanish appetizer thoroughly before serving. Dice the vegetables fine and then mix all ingredients. Go easy with the tabasco.

Lamb Curry (India)

1   lb lamb stew meat
1   onion, chopped
1   green pepper, chopped
½   cup celery, cut in 1" pieces

1　*large carrot, cut up*
1　*apple, peeled and diced*
½　*TB curry powder*
½　*tsp salt*
¼　*tsp garlic salt*

If you've not tried this before, go easy on the curry powder, for it's a taste you sort of have to acquire. Brown the meat first and then push to one side of the fry pan. Add the onion, celery, green pepper and garlic salt and sauté for a couple of minutes. Add the curry and cook a few more minutes. Add the rest of the ingredients, mix everything with the meat, and add a little water to keep the mixture moist. Cover and simmer until the meat is tender. Serve with rice.

Norwegian Meatballs

1　*lb hamburger*
1　*egg*
½　*cup milk*
1　*cup bread crumbs*
1　*TB finely minced onion*
1½　*cups beef bouillon*
¼　*tsp nutmeg*
　　salt and pepper

For a truly international meal, try this with spaghetti Italiano and American spaghetti sauce. Sauté the onions gently. Mix bread crumbs and milk, then mix all the ingredients together (except the bouillon), and shape into small balls about 1 inch in diameter. Brown the meatballs on all sides. Heat the bouillon in a deep pot, add the browned meatballs, and simmer for half an hour.

Sweet and Sour Pork (China)

1 *lb pork shoulder, cut in strips*
1 *can pineapple chunks (save juice)*
1 *onion, thinly sliced*
1 *green pepper, thinly sliced*
⅓ *cup vinegar*
¼ *cup brown sugar*
2 *TB cornstarch*
1 *TB soy sauce*
½ *tsp salt*
½ *cup water*

They say the Chinese invented just about everything, but even if they didn't, this one dish ought to
endear them to you forever. Brown the pork. Add
vinegar, brown sugar, salt, soy sauce and pineapple
juice, and cook covered over low heat for 30 minutes, or
until meat is tender. Blend the cornstarch with the ½ cup
water and stir into the meat mixture until it thickens,
about 2 minutes. Add the green pepper, onion and
pineapple chunks, and cook another 2 or 3 minutes.
Serve with or over rice.

Toad in a Hole (England)

6 *link sausages*
batch of biscuit dough (see p. 104)

Don't let the name of this old English dish turn you
off: it's really delicious. Make up the biscuit dough as
directed and cut out the biscuits. Wrap each sausage link
in a biscuit so that only about ¼ inch of sausage
protrudes at each end. Pop in the oven and bake, along
with the rest of the "unsausaged" biscuits, at 425° for
about 15 minutes, or until the biscuits are brown.

Desserts

J*E*L*L*O

1   box J*E*L*L*O   1   cup cold water
1   cup boiling water

Pick your favorite color and dissolve in a pan containing the boiling water. Add the cold water and stir about. Pour into four individual cups or bowls, and stick in the refrig. Simple, huh? Any idiot can do this, so go to it. Spice it up by adding some fruit cocktail when it's about half jelled, and top with whipped or sour cream.

Ices and Sherbets

ICES:

Flavor	Juice (cups)	Sugar (cups)	Water (cups)
Lemon	1	2	4
Grape	2 grape 1/4 lemon	2	2
Orange	2 orange 1/4 lemon	2	3
Pineapple	2 1/2 cups crushed pineapple 1/2 cup lemon juice	2	2

You really should use fresh fruit for the lemon and orange ices, but the canned or bottled stuff will do. Mix everything together until the sugar dissolves. Freeze in the freezing compartment of your refrigerator.

SHERBETS:

Use any recipe for an ice, making the mix slightly sweeter and stronger in flavor. When the mixture is partially frozen, stir in 2 stiffly beaten egg whites and complete the freezing.

Chocolate and Butterscotch Pie

First the crust:
     1½   *cups all-purpose flour*

To make acorn coffee, take sound ripe acorns, peel them and roast them with a little butter or fat, then, when cold, grind them with one third their weight of real coffee.

½ *cup lard or vegetable shortening*
5-6 *TB cold water*

Sift the flour and salt together, then cut in the lard or shortening and mix with a fork, or use your fingers. Mix in the water, a bit at a time, until the dough forms a ball that is neither sticky nor crumbly. Refrigerate for 10 to 15 minutes before rolling. Cut the ball of dough in two (this recipe makes two 9-inch crusts), and roll out on a floured board to a ⅛-inch thickness about 9 inches in diameter. Fold one half of the crust over the other and place in the pie tin, then unfold, and with fingers form crust to fit pan, pressing down the edges on the rim of the pan with a fork. Bake at 450° for 15 minutes, or until brown.

Then the filling:
      box chocolate pudding   1
1   *box butterscotch pudding*

Prepare each flavor separately according to directions on the box, then pour into the baked pie shells. Let 'em cool for a bit, then chill in the refrigerator. If you like, you can add a little whipped cream when serving.

Doughnuts

2½ *cups all-purpose flour*
1 *egg, beaten*
½ *cup sugar*
½ *cup milk*
1 *TB shortening, melted*
½ *tsp salt*
   dash of nutmeg
   dash of cinnamon
2 *tsp baking powder*

Mix flour, baking powder and spices. In a separate bowl, mix egg, sugar, salt and melted shortening, and to this add the milk and the flour mixture just enough to blend. Roll the dough ⅓ to ½ inch thick on a floured board, and cut out doughnuts. Fry in deep fat which has been heated to 375° until brown on both sides. Drain on paper towels. This'll give you about a dozen doughnuts. Save a couple to dunk in your coffee tomorrow morning.

Oatmeal Cookies

     2   cups rolled oats
     ¾   cup sugar
     ½   cup butter or margarine, melted
     ¼   cup flour
     2   egg whites, stiffly beaten

Anybody who doesn't like oatmeal cookies or peanut butter is un-American! And they're not exactly a dessert—they're for tea time or a midnight snack or to dunk in your coffee for breakfast. Anyway, to make 'em

Facts We Can't Prove. *Mixing eggs in a copper bowl will make the lightest, fluffiest omelets, soufflés, meringues, angel food and sponge cakes. A unique chemical reaction with the egg whites is supposed to give them twice the volume. We found this one in a* **Hard To Find Tools** *book. The bowl only cost 17 bucks, and anyhow, it's good to shave with.*

is easy. In a mixing bowl stir together the oats, sugar, butter and flour. Fold in the egg whites until well blended. Drop by heaping teaspoonfuls on greased cookie sheets. Bake in preheated 350° oven until they turn golden brown, which is about 12 minutes.

Strawberry Shortcake

1   *pt fresh strawberries*
    baking powder biscuits (see p. 104)
½   *cup sugar*
    whipped cream (optional)

Some people get hives from strawberries, and if that's your case, it's just T.S. Pick and wash the berries first, then crush ever so gently in a bowl and then mix in the sugar. Chill in the refrigerator for at least 2 hours, but overnight is better. Make the biscuits as directed. For each serving, halve 2 hot biscuits, cover with the berries and top with whipped cream.

Rice Pudding

⅓   *cup rice*   ½   *tsp salt*
4   *cups milk*   ½   *cup raisins*
⅓   *cup sugar*

To Test Nutmegs. *Prick them with a pin. If good, the oil will immediately spread around the puncture.*

This is another oldie that's been around so long that it was probably invented by the Chinese. Wash the rice and then mix everything together. Pour into a greased baking dish and bake at 250° (slow oven) for about 3 hours. Stir the pudding occasionally during the first hour. Serve plain or with cream.

Bread Pudding

4	slices stale bread		6	TB sugar
1	TB butter or margarine			pinch of salt
2	eggs, slightly beaten		2	cups milk
½	cup raisins (optional)		½	tsp vanilla

This pudding is so old-fashioned it's practically been forgotten, but for those who've eaten it, it's still as tasty as ever. Butter the bread and cut into ½-inch cubes and place in a baking dish. Mix the rest of the stuff together and pour over the bread. Set the baking dish in a pan of hot water and bake for 40 minutes at 350°.

Tapioca Pudding

8	TB granular tapioca		2	TB honey
3	cups milk		1	tsp vanilla

To Banish Rats from the Premises. *Use pounded glass mixed with dry cornmeal, placed within their reach. Sprinkling cayenne pepper in their holes will also banish them.*

This is another old-fashioned dessert that is rarely served anymore, despite its simplicity to make and tasty flavor. Soak the tapioca in the milk for 15 minutes. Cook over medium heat until thickened, about 8 to 10 minutes. Do not overcook. Stir in vanilla and honey. Let set until cool and then chill in refrigerator.

Brown Betty

2	cups soft bread crumbs
4	TB butter or margarine
3	cups pared, sliced apples
½	cup sugar
¼	tsp cinnamon
1½	tsp lemon juice
¼	cup water

This old dessert predates the American Revolution and has always been a poor man's sweet. Melt the butter and then pour over the bread crumbs and mix. In a greased baking dish, place ⅓ of the crumbs. Add a layer consisting of ½ of the apples, sugar, cinnamon, water and lemon juice. Repeat this process and top with the remaining ⅓ of the crumbs. Bake covered for 30 minutes at 375°. Remove the cover and bake for another 30 minutes. Serve with cream.

To remove corns on the feet, roast a clove of garlic on a live coal in hot ashes, apply it to the corn, and fasten it with a piece of cloth on going to bed.

Stewed Apricots

⅓ lb dried apricots   2 to 3 cups water
¼ cup sugar

As a dessert, serve with cream or over ice cream. For breakfast, mix with dried cereal and milk. Simmer the fruit in water until tender. Add the sugar and cook until dissolved. If syrup is too thin, remove fruit and boil juice until it thickens.

Baked Apples

4 apples, cored   juice of 1 lemon
   sugar

This dessert is cheap and tasty and can also be served cold for breakfast. Place the apples in a baking dish, fill the core cavities with sugar, and a few drops of lemon juice. Pour an inch of water into the baking dish and bake at 375° until soft. Baste each apple 3 or 4 times while baking. Serve hot.

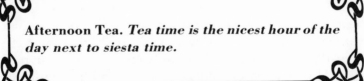

Afternoon Tea. *Tea time is the nicest hour of the day next to siesta time.*

Booze and Other Beverages

BOOZE MAKING

Strictly speaking this really isn't a cookbook item, but considering the fact that the guys and chicks for whom this book was written are usually short of bread, and the fact that booze is a pretty important part of an artist's diet, the publisher agreed to include this chapter on homemade sauce as a public service.

Biggest problem in making booze is how to eliminate or disguise the odor of cooking mash or fermenting raisin jack in order to keep the landlord or fuzz off your back. You can stash your crocks of raisin jack or mash on the roof to ferment, but cooking it off up there is a mite risky. A top floor pad at least six flights up is the best place for brewing, because it not only provides good ventilation but few fat fuzz will climb that high to investigate, and the landlord only comes around on rent day. Always do your cooking at night with the lights off and don't answer any knocks at the door.

Precautionary Note: Best have a friend who works at a medical lab run off a test on a sample batch before getting juiced. If this isn't possible, invite a friend over and give him a small belt and watch for any untoward results.

Coconut Delight

1	*coconut*	1	*dozen raisins (more or less)*
1	*TB sugar*	1	*cork*

The more coconuts you buy, the more jolts you get. Be sure to get a female nut (one full of milk). Knock out the bunghole, pour in the sugar and raisins, cork it back up. Set it in a convenient warm corner of the pad and wait. In from three days to a week it'll blow its cork and you'll have a tasty cup of juice, man.

Iced Water

1	*pitcher water* *ice cubes*

You can always put something into your complaining stomach as long as there's a water tap around. And this least expensive item in your *Guide to Better and Cheaper Cooking* is both versatile and beneficial. It's not only great to dull hunger and quench thirst with, but it just can't be beat for chasing down scotch and other boozes. As a remedy for alleviating hangover fires, it's in a class by itself. Bottle it, man, and keep stocked in the refrig! Also great for taking aspirin, vitamins, and other nourishing (and nonnourishing) pills.

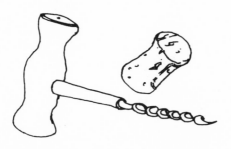

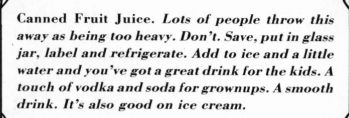

Canned Fruit Juice. *Lots of people throw this away as being too heavy. Don't. Save, put in glass jar, label and refrigerate. Add to ice and a little water and you've got a great drink for the kids. A touch of vodka and soda for grownups. A smooth drink. It's also good on ice cream.*

Wine, *Vino*

1	*2-3 gal plastic pail*
1	*gal glass jug*
	piece of cheesecloth
	plastic wrap
1	*large paper bag*
4	*lb fruit, cut up*
¼	*oz package of dry active yeast*
1	*slice cold toast*
5	*orange slices*
4	*lemon slices*
4	*qts water*
1	*rubber band*

Making wine is really very simple, says a wine-making artist buddy, whose cellar looks a little like a lab. In bumming around the world we've tasted some really great homemade stuff. Particularly fruit wines and brandies. These are for the most part made by people who have been making them for years. Each, of course, has his or her well-hidden formula. This is that rare stuff you'll never be buying in any liquor store. Take it from me, some of it is really potent.

Take about 4 pounds of cut-up fruit, wash well. Blueberries, strawberries, apples, peaches, apricots, cherries, pineapples—any of these will do for a try. Put fruit into the pail with sugar, water, orange and lemon slices. Stir with water till all the sugar is dissolved. Dilute the yeast in a bowl of lukewarm water, and put piece of dry toast in this. Turn till all the liquid is absorbed. Float toast in fruit mixture, cover with cheese-cloth and let sit for 4 to 5 days. Siphon off liquid, leaving sediment on bottom of pail. Remove the sediment wrapped in cheesecloth, and press out remaining juice into jar. Cover with plastic bag secured with rubber band. Put a pinhole in plastic cover. Cover whole jar with paper bag to keep out light, and wait till wine stops bubbling. About 4 weeks or so. Bottle it, Daddy, it's all yours. If it's bad, can always be used for vinegar.

NOTE: The best source for wine is grape, since it is the only fruit that has everything: natural yeast, sugar, juice and acids. The natural yeast converts the sugar to alcohol and carbon dioxide; the carbon dioxide dissipates into air; and the alcohol kills the yeast! What is left is *vino*! The hardest parts are: when to pick the grapes (no job for a novice), fermentation, timing, temperature control, and crushing and pressing the grapes. Not to mention the whole process of bottling and storage. Simple! We do have some recipes. If you are interested drop us a line at the publisher's, and we will pass them along. About 18 pounds of grapes will give you one gallon of wine, depending on the grapes. . . .

Laws. You'll need a permit to make wine. Get a Form 1541 from the Bureau of Alcohol, Tobacco and Firearms, and mail to Regional Director of the Bureau in New York, Chicago, Philadelphia, San Francisco, Cincinnati, Atlanta or Dallas. Some states—New Jersey and Texas (Texans drink wine?)—require you to register with their bureaus.

Only heads of families are allowed to make wine at

home. Those of you who live alone are excluded. Discrimination, if you ask me. A person need not be married to qualify as the head of the family (that's nice), but you must have one other person living in your home. (That's nicer.) The person must be related to you by blood, marriage or adoption. (So adopt a mate.) The wine must be for your family use only, and the maximum is 200 gallons per year. (That's one helluva lot of *vino*.) The law also says that you must register at least 5 days before you start running your still. Once you apply and receive a permit, you need never register again. (They got your name, kiddo, and you're on the CIA list for life.) See your Congressman! You'll also have to file an annual report on the amount you made, and you can't move it from the premises without written permission. On second thought, hell with the whole thing!

The Hard Stuff

NOTE: Legally, beer and whiskey can be made only on licensed and taxed premises, such as a brewery or distillery. So, start a brewery or distillery.

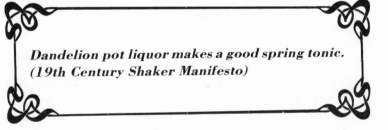

Dandelion pot liquor makes a good spring tonic.
(19th Century Shaker Manifesto)

Catalog

If you are interested in a list of fine Paperback
books, covering a wide range of subjects
and interests, send your name and address,
requesting your free catalog, to:

McGraw-Hill Paperbacks
1221 Avenue of Americas
New York, N. Y. 10020